D1456548

THE
FOURTH
MEGA-MARKET

THE FOURTH MEGA-MARKET

NOW THROUGH 2011

HOW THREE EARLIER BULL MARKETS EXPLAIN THE PRESENT AND PREDICT THE FUTURE

RALPH ACAMPORA

WITH MICHAEL D'ANTONIO

HYPERION

NEW YORK

Copyright © 2000 Ralph Acampora

Photo credit page 159: Francis Miller, *Life* magazine, copyright © Time, Inc.

Charts prepared by The Graphic Source, Inc.

Designed by Michael Mendelsohn

Library of Congress Cataloging-in-Publication Data
Acampora, Ralph.
  The fourth mega-market, now through 2011: how three earlier bull markets explain the present and predict the future / Ralph Acampora—1st ed.
    p. cm.
  ISBN: 0-7868-6651-9
  1. Investments—United States. 2. Stocks—United States. 3. Economic forecasting—United States. 4. United States—Economic conditions—1981–
I. Title.
HG4910 .A625 2000
332.64'273—dc21   00-04084

FIRST EDITION

10   9   8   7   6   5   4   3   2   1

"AMO LA STORIA. LEGGI LA TUTTA.
IMPARERAI DELLA STORIA."

—*Teresa Fusco Acampora*

These are the words I heard
over and over again as a young boy.
It was my dear mother
who taught me to love history;
to read all of it; and to learn from it.

CONTENTS

THE
FOURTH
MEGA-MARKET

FOREWORD

IN THE LAST FEW YEARS countless newspaper articles, magazine pieces, and even books have celebrated the long-term bull market that began in the mid-1990s. So much has been published that the genre has become a cottage industry.

While each book and article may be slightly different, they all follow the same basic format. The author begins by offering explanations for the market's remarkable rise, and then he gets to the main point. The party has only begun, he declares. Then he goes on to predict extremely optimistic upside targets for the Dow Jones Industrial average.

Not surprisingly, each writer tries to outdo the last when it comes to predicting how high the market could go. We have been told that the Dow will hit 36,000, 40,000, and even the 100,000 level within the next two decades.

I confess that I enjoy reading these predictions. After all, for those of us who invest in stocks, they offer wonderful news. Our equity holdings are going to be worth a lot more if these forecasters are right.

And I honestly hope that they do turn out to be correct, especially for my friends in the business who have gone out of their way to predict the Dow will hit a certain number by a certain time.

I won't do it. (Though I admit Dow 1,024,683 has a nice ring to it.) This is not because I am not bullish. I am. But I am a prudent bull. I know bear markets. I know that there are bear markets, and we must always be on guard because they are very painful. And I also know that pegging the exact peak of a bull market is one thing, finding out why it could get there is another. Knowing the why and how is a far more important thing for me.

In fact, while we make predictions, no one can guarantee the immediate future of the market. This is why I have to offer you a very serious and prudent warning, right up front. All bull markets, including the mega-markets I am writing about, undergo sharp drops along their way to a peak. Such periodic washouts are common and are necessary for a mega-market to be sustainable over the long term. Bear markets help undo the excesses — a time to prune the tree, so to speak. Knowing that these interruptions or nasty corrections or even bear markets occur allows an investor to be better prepared.

Indeed, understanding the market is far more important than the predictions that can be bought for the price of a magazine or newspaper. So instead of throwing out Kreskin-like statements about the future, I will share my vision of how the market works, so that you can understand the extraordinary times we live in and make your own assessment.

I will explain the primary reasons why many stocks have climbed so dramatically in recent years. And I'll explain, in detail, why I believe stocks still have a long way to run.

This second point is extremely important. As the market has continued its relentless drive upward during the last five years or so, too many have gotten out too early. When the market hit 5,000 or 8,000, they were convinced that stocks could not go any higher, and they sold.

I began researching the market's unusual strength in early 1995, when the Dow was still in the low 4,000s. At that time I realized that several key economic and political factors were coming together in such a way that could create an environment that would support a multiyear stock market rise. After checking my facts, and checking them again, I predicted that the Dow would hit 7,000.

Dow 7,000 may not sound like the stratosphere today, but it was 60 percent above the market's level at that time. And I said it would make the jump within the coming three years.

Not surprisingly, my analysis met with a lot of skepticism. People who were trying to be kind said I was being overly optimistic. Those who were not so kind simply said I was nuts.

Just about the only thing everyone agreed on was that my career was balanced on that bold prediction. If I was right, and my company invested accordingly, I would be a hero. If I turned out to be wrong, my career would be over. Thirty years on Wall Street, thirty years of building a reputation, would be squandered.

In the seasons that followed my initial analysis — the famous Dow 7,000 call—I had to write several reports to our clients defending my forecast. These were especially important whenever the market stopped its steady rise and suffered a reversal. I had to reassure people that while there would be corrections along the way, the bull market would continue. In the summer of 1998, for example, the Dow Jones Industrial average fell 19.5 percent. It was 21.5 percent if you included intra-day highs and lows, and that meant we were officially in a cyclical bear market, something that happens if stock prices fall 20 percent or more in a few months. But in special bulletins to our clients, I urged them to stay the course and explained why. Most did.

At other points, drops of 2 percent, 3 percent, and even 4 percent in a single day seemed to become commonplace. I argued then that if you hung in there, you would be rewarded. The overall direction would be dramatically higher. For those with long-term views of the market, this meant the good times should continue.

As time, hard work, and a little luck would have it, my prediction of Dow 7,000 came true in February 1997. In subsequent letters to our clients I explained in detail why I thought that stocks would continue their climb. Of course, naysayers still challenged me, and at that point I spent a long time wrestling with the data to be sure that conditions had not changed. It was no surprise to me and to our clients when the Dow hit the 10,000 mark in March 1999.

The market was being driven upward by a somewhat narrower group of industries and this would present a problem later on. But there were powerful positive forces in place, and it seemed clear to me that stocks wanted to move higher — a lot higher.

I could be somewhat certain of what the data said, but I wanted to understand better what was happening on a human level. The market is, after all, driven by human beings, and that is what makes it endlessly fascinating.

I dug deeper and deeper into history for the answers. This research, which became the foundation for this book, has taken me into areas I never explored before, such as defense spending and the biological sciences, to name just two. But these subjects are vitally important, if you truly want to understand why the market will be heading substantially higher.

The single most important new fact I came to understand is that, contrary to what everyone seems to believe, the current bull market is not "unprecedented." In fact, what we are living through has occurred three times before in our history, and each time stocks have climbed dramatically. We are right in the middle of what I have come to call the fourth great mega-market.

If history holds — and I am convinced it will — stocks will continue to climb higher during what is now the fourth mega-market. I am coining the phrase "mega-market" to describe a bull market that runs about a decade or more. During mega-markets we can expect to see gains of at least 400 percent to 500 percent over a period that can last anywhere from ten to seventeen years. But remember there will be corrections and these are an integral part of a mega-market.

The world doesn't need another book by some guy yelling about how he made a million dollars — and you can too. I prefer to explain, to teach. And, if I do my job right, three things will happen as you read this book. (Don't worry, all of them are good.)

- First, you will learn that technical analysis — the method I use to examine the stock market — is not for traders only. You can use it for making your own long-term forecasts. (I'll show you how.) And you'll see that true research should incorporate all the disciplines of analysis: economic, fundamental, quantitative, and technical. Used together, they will increase the odds that you will be a successful investor.
- Second, you'll come to understand the effect that history has on our stock market and see that the world in which we are living is not unprecedented — as many people have argued.
- Third, you will recognize that we are right in the middle of the fourth great bull market in American history. Armed with a thorough understanding of what drives markets — including emotional *and* technical causes — you should be able to chart your own course to the future. You will be prepared to spot the signs of corrections and bear markets, and you will know the steps you can take to avoid them.

Though many are reluctant to declare it, we are once again living in a golden age. America in the early 2000s is ascendant. The advances we see in medicine and information technology are astonishing. It's no wonder that the stock market is as volatile as it is. This is an inflection point in history, a time of major changes in the way we live and the way we conduct business; hence stock prices will gyrate in response to wild expectations and inevitable failures.

The market is a roller coaster, both terrifying and exhilarating. Buckle up, it's going to be an exciting and breath-taking ride.

RALPH J. ACAMPORA
NEW YORK
SUMMER 2000

CHAPTER 1

OUT OF THE BOX

Y OU KNOW, you should write this down."
It was October 2, 1997, and I was having breakfast with my
boss, Hardwick "Wick" Simmons, chairman of Prudential Securities.
Our conversation meandered around many topics but it always
returned to the stock market. We marveled at how rewarding the previous couple of years had been for all those who were willing to take
a risk in equities. The Dow had gone from 3,600 to 8,300 over that
time. Wick kept talking about risk and what it meant to the firm's
clients. Those who had been willing to go along with the firm's recommendations, and assumed a modicum of risk, had made a lot of
money.

This reminded me that Prudential had taken risks too, on me.
I thanked Wick for being willing to stake the firm's reputation on
my research. I reminded him of how proud I was when our firm
allowed me to publish what appeared to be an outrageous report
(forecasting Dow 7,000) back in June 1995. Prudential and its
clients had depended on my risk assessment to invest enormous
sums of money. They had been rewarded with a doubling in the
market.

This was the point at which Wick told me I should "write this down." At first I didn't quite understand what he was saying. He explained himself bluntly.

"I think you should write a book."

I was flabbergasted. "Why in the world would anyone want that?" I asked.

"Well, all of *us* are curious about what made you 'step out of the box' and write that bullish report. Some of us still don't know what made you do it. I think a lot of people would want to know what you were thinking about. What did you see that nobody else did?"

I hesitated for a moment. While I had thought about writing a book, I had never let myself say it out loud. "Well," I said, "there really is a story behind this story. It's got something to do with me personally — the books I like to read and the intellectual discipline I developed during my years in a Catholic seminary. But mostly it's about history and about technical analysis."

"Then do it," Wick told me.

TIMING

I can honestly say that I have dedicated most of my professional career to proselytizing for technical analysis. For example, this Monday night, just like on every other Monday night for the last three decades, you will be able to find me in classroom 8 at the New York Institute of Finance teaching the basic course in technical analysis. That doesn't surprise anyone who knows me even casually. I have a mission. I will convince the financial community that technical research is a legitimate form of stock market analysis.

This fire in my belly was ignited in the mid-1960s when I was first introduced to charting, something that we will explore in detail in later chapters. Once I truly understood how to use the charts that are the core of technical analysis, I realized my career in investment research was not doomed because of a lack of education in fundamental analysis and traditional economic theories. (My college degree was in history and political science. In the seminary I had worked toward a Master's in theology.) I began to think that I might be able to make a living on Wall Street after all.

Don't get me wrong. All forms of research are needed to do a credible job of determining how individual stocks should be valued. But technical analysis provides a critical element — timing. We technicians are market timers. We try to determine when to get into (buy) and out of (sell) a stock.

Fundamental analysts research and create important numbers (earnings, revenues, price/earnings multiples, etc.) and then tell you where they think the stock should go based on their findings. They compare a company to its competitors and try to gauge whether its price is a good value. The idea, to oversimplify, is to buy a good stock, at let's say $20 a share, and hold on to it for a while and presumably sell it years later for $60.

Now, in the process of climbing to $60, that stock may go to $40, then back down to $25, before it eventually rises to $60. But by the time you sell, the proponents of this approach argue, you will have a nice $40 profit.

Market timers don't have any quarrel with making $40 on a $20 stock. But we try to do better. Our goal, again to oversimplify, is to buy that stock at $20, and then sell it when it is rising, say, at $37.

Now wait, you might say. You missed the run-up to $40. That's true. But we also missed the drop back down. If fact, we might take our profits and reinvest in the same issue at $27, during its fall to $25. If our technical analysis is correct, we'll ride up again to say $57. Yes, we might not ride the stock all the way up. But the important thing is we don't ride it all the way back down.

This approach takes a bit more work on our part, and it's not for people who can't pay constant attention to their portfolios. But in our fictional example we end with a $47 gain, instead of $40. That's a 17.5 percent greater return (before factoring in commissions).

As I've said, I don't think there is anything wrong with fundamental analysis. In fact, if I could do my formal education over, I would love to be an economist — one trained in the fundamentals — with a technical bias. Unfortunately, many economists and fundamental analysts do not recognize the value of technical analysis.

Traditionally most people in academia and on Wall Street were never taught technical analysis. The reason is that very few colleges or universities actually offer the subject to their students. This is because most academics believe in the efficient market hypothesis — that is, they believe that all information that could move a stock price is known to just about everyone simultaneously. They argue that since news about a company's sales, earnings, marketing efforts, or technical snafus is communicated just about instantly to everyone, it is impossible for one person to see a trend earlier than anyone else. To them, it's impossible to anticipate a market turn, and technical analysis is useless.

Historically, the academy has attacked the notion of anyone being able successfully to time the market with any regularity. But the success of many market timers has caught the attention of more open-minded professors and investors. Our reputation is improving rapidly, and credible research is being done that shows you can successfully use price momentum to time the market.

As I write, a historic alliance is being formed by the Market Technicians Association, the official organization for technicians, and a very highly respected business school on the East Coast. (I'll give you a hint. It's a member of the Ivy League.) Together they are in the early stages of setting up a center for research into technical analysis. Great news indeed, not only for technicians but for all serious students and investors alike.

But, in the words of one of the professors at that prestigious school: "There is one problem. The word 'technical' has a black eye!" This is true. Too many tenured professors will not accept the word "technical," but they are now willing to research the concept, convinced that the underlying ideas have validity. These newly enlightened professors feel more comfortable with the phrase "behavioral analysis."

My guess is whatever we end up calling the center it will have "behavioral analysis" in the official name. As far as I am concerned, you can call it what you want. What is important is that more and more people will get to understand the technical factors that govern the market's performance. This is a breakthrough that I would have had trouble imagining back in the early years of my career, when I began to believe what history and data were telling me.

THE MOST DIFFICULT MARKET

The year was 1970, and I was part of a scorned breed, scorned at least on Wall Street. People who did what I did — recommending stocks based on historical price patterns — were literally laughed at by many of the Street's citizens. I couldn't accept this. I talked this over with two new friends, John Brooks and John Greeley at the brokerage firm of Francis I. Dupont and Co., who like me were succeeding with technical analysis. We knew it worked and, in an effort to improve the credibility of our methods, we started talking about creating a trade association for technicians. It would be a way for us to meet, share thoughts, and compare ideas, the way other Wall Street professionals did.

To raise our profile, we enlisted the help of the two top names in our field, Robert "Bob" Farrell at Merrill Lynch, Pierce, Fenner & Smith and my boss, Alan R. Shaw of Harris Upham and Co., which is now part of what is known as Salomon Smith Barney. After much debate over whether or not we would actually get taken seriously enough to create what would be the first national organization of technicians, we decided to give it a try. And then Alan suggested something that was as daunting to me as starting the association itself.

"You know, of course, you'll have to get the blessing of the Old Man."

I didn't need to ask whom he meant. The Old Man was Ken Ward of Hayden Stone and Co. At the time, he was one of the oldest living technicians. Mr. Ward was close to seventy years old. He had seen it all, from the Roaring 1920s and the Crash of 1929 to the Great Depression, World War II, and the long bull market of the 1960s.

Alan was right, of course; we would need Ken Ward's support. So after working up my nerve, I called him on the phone. At first he told me in a clipped, serious voice, that any campaign to improve the image of technicians would fail. He called me "young man," and said we would never be taken seriously. There were too many obstacles. It was too soon. People weren't ready to believe that you could actually determine how the market and individual stocks would behave in the future based on stock charts and analysis of their past performance.

But of course I was young and wouldn't take no for an answer. Both John Brooks and I kept pushing and finally Ken did agree to participate. But he required two things in trade. First, every member would have to be a technical analyst who followed equities — corporate stocks — not commodities. Second, he or she had to be the author of a technical market letter sent to clients or be the writer of technical reports that were sent to portfolio managers at an investment management firm.

Ken Ward was determined that our members be working for either an established Wall Street brokerage firm or an investment company where the firm had to be taking them seriously enough to let them make recommendations to clients. In the end, we could find only eighteen people who met those requirements at the time. Together we became the Market Technicians Association (MTA).

At our first meeting, I finally got to meet Ken Ward in person. This, for me, was the equivalent of meeting my childhood baseball idol, Joe DiMaggio. Ken Ward had lived through most of the bull and bear markets of the century. I wanted to know everything he had learned from this experience.

I asked him, "Mr. Ward, what was the most difficult market you ever experienced?" And as I asked the question I remember feeling really stupid. I anticipated his response and said, "Of course, it was the Crash of 1929." Then he surprised me with his answer.

"No, kid. That was a layup. The toughest market I ever saw, by far, was the one from 1962 to 1966. If you go through something like that, it will be the roughest thing you'll ever experience."

I did a double take.

"But the market went up during that time" I blurted out. "It was a steep bull market that went on for several years. In fact, between 1962 and 1966 didn't the Dow go up about 75 percent?"

"That's right, kid," Ken Ward replied. "It went up and up and up, and rolled right over all of us, bulls and bears alike. Nobody believed it. And it made us look like fools."

As he talked I realized just how remarkable that climb had been. That bull market continued, on and on, despite events that could have crippled it, including: the Cuban Missile Crisis, President Kennedy's assassination, and President Johnson's heart attack.

THE SECULAR BULL MARKET IN THE EARLY 1960s

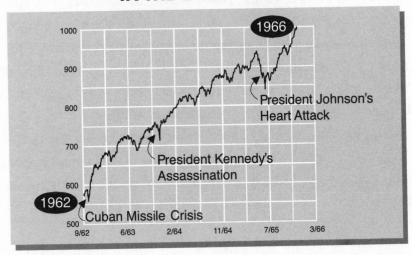

"The biggest mistake we all made was that we sold the good-looking stocks too early," Ken Ward continued. "It was a time of vicious rotation [when investors move out of one sector and into another], very vicious rotation, and a time when one really had to believe that we were in a secular bull market to benefit, and very few of us were able to understand that we were, in fact, in a secular bull market."

Ken Ward was absolutely right. The market he was describing had gone way up and rolled over everyone. From June 1962 through January 1966, a period of three and a half years, the Dow Jones Industrials climbed 75 percent. Impressive indeed.

But the increase of that market, from 1962 to 1966, was only a tiny fraction of the bull market we've seen recently. Between November 1994 and today, in early 2000, the Dow rose more than 200 percent. Unfortunately for many, many people on Wall Street, and even for many technical analysts, this bull market did the same thing that the bull market of the 1960s did to Ken Ward and his colleagues.

It has rolled over all the bears and even the bulls. The market made the careers of those who chose not to fight the trend, but it destroyed the reputations of those on Wall Street who chose to fight it.

As a technical analyst I watch the market. The entire market. And by tracking individual stocks (the bottom up approach) I can assess the direction of not only groups, but of the market as a whole. Why do I devote this much attention to such details? Because the most important thing to an individual investor is his or her specific portfolio.

I know from my many years of experience that you also have to take a top-down approach (study overall indicators and indices). Once you have established to your satisfaction that you are either in a bull or bear market, then you can trade accordingly. Deciding where you think the market is going to go is an important first step because you need to think and act differently in a bull market than you do when you expect the market to be bearish.

Naturally, every type of analyst tries to predict the future. Fundamentalists focus on the earnings of companies within specific sectors. Quantitative analysts (a.k.a. the quants) take the numbers generated by all the fundamentalists and back test them for all sectors and all companies. They try to explain whether a company is overvalued or undervalued relative to itself, to its peers, and to the overall market.

In contrast, we technicians plot and study a different set of numbers — price and volume — and read the resulting charts in light of important historical factors. We watch trends in actual trading: Has a stock been steadily rising or falling in price? And then we look for the exceptions and ask ourselves: Is the trend changing? We search for recurring price patterns, and increases or decreases in volume. We respect market psychology and live by the dictum that buyers (demand) push stock prices up while sellers (supply) force stock prices lower.

This dictum is absolute. It implies that someone out there knows more about the company in question than we do. And if enough of these "informed investors" decide to buy or sell on information that we do not have, then we must respect their action.

This bias — that the marketplace includes wise buyers and sellers — results in the old adage: "Don't fight the tape." If enough investors want a specific stock, or the market in general, to go higher, it will, regardless of what any one individual thinks is right. In this situation, technicians believe it is better to get on the moving train than to stand in front of it.

We technicians also look at recurring factors such as presidential cycles, and seasonal events such as year-end rallies. I personally take one more giant step and ask "why?" I accept without questioning that a certain trend is unfolding — I have no intention of getting in front of a moving train — but I insist on finding out what is causing prices to move.

Understanding the cause will help me anticipate how long a trend may last. It's hard to overemphasize how different this approach is from the typical Wall Street bias. The "establishment" on the Street actually does the opposite of what I do. They predict where the market should go based on their estimates of value, earnings per share, and the like, and then complain when the market doesn't respond the way they think it should or does something that they can't explain. Quite often they wind up fighting the tape, or to use another image, they get trampled by a rampaging bull.

A MARKET THAT WANTS TO GO UP

Let's examine a specific case. Back in March 1995, when this wild ride started, the market was showing me something I had never seen before. The Dow was at 4,200, after having climbed 500 points — or nearly 17 percent — in the previous three months.

Though a 17 percent rise in three months may not startle anyone today, it was only the second time in the thirty years I'd been in the business that I'd seen the Dow gain 500 points in such a short period of time. (The first time was during the Persian Gulf War when the Dow Industrials went from 2,470.30 on January 9, 1991, to 2,972.50 on March 5, 1991: a 20.3 percent gain.)

But here we had a situation that showed all the signs of topping that gain by a wide margin. The market had already gone up 17 percent and showed no sign of slowing down.

What made the advance in 1995 even more surprising was that it was being done against a backdrop of news that normally would have been considered devastating. We had just gone through the Orange County, California, bond crisis in 1994, in which the once-wealthy county had defaulted on its bonds. Defaults on municipal bonds are incredibly rare and this one, because of its size, sent shock waves across the country. At the same time the Mexican economy was going bankrupt, and as a direct result of our country's effort to help, the U.S. dollar collapsed. And, finally, we had the Barings Securities scandal in Singapore and London, where a major international banking firm was brought to its knees.

And yet, despite all of this, the market kept going up. And I could not forget the old technician's refrain: "When bad news can't take the market down, it is good news."

Clearly in the early spring of 1995 the market was demonstrating to me that it was strong, very strong, in spite of all these negative factors, any one of which normally would have been enough to send the market lower. Here we had three potentially disastrous events, and not only didn't the market fall, it kept climbing.

Other analysts, who considered only the macro, or big picture, indicators, were all predicting a quick end to the rally. Macro indicators provide a top-down view of the world of Wall Street. And in 1995 they were not indicating that anything out of the ordinary was going on.

But there is a second way to scrutinize the scene — the bottom-up, or micro, approach, which deals solely with the movement of individual stock prices. In my micro analysis I uncovered a bevy of technically attractive stocks to recommend — name brands like Coca-Cola, GE, and McDonald's — even though the Dow had already gained 500 quick points, a remarkable move back then. (One company, Vitesse Semiconductors, was a mere $7 stock; it looked like it could at least triple.)

Confronted with some negative macro indicators and highly positive micro indicators, I was faced with a dilemma. Should I believe my market data — the macro indicators — or should I accept as true what certainly appeared to be a rising tide of demand for stocks?

I thought about this for a long time. Everyone else was saying that the run we had had in stocks was over. If I said it wasn't, I certainly would get attention. But if I were wrong I would have damaged my credibility.

As part of my soul-searching I recalled my first conversation with Ken Ward in 1970. Back then he had said that the biggest mistake you can make in a powerful bull market is to sell good-looking stocks too early. And he was certainly right about that. But he also said something else. He told me "rotation is the lifeline of a bull market."

And it was clear that the market in mid-1995 was undergoing massive rotation, with people riding one sector up for a while, and then switching into another and driving that sector higher as well. The more I thought about it, the more I was convinced that the micro approach — the technical factors that show how individual stocks are doing, as opposed to the macro-indicators that govern the entire market —were right.

Then and there I adopted the following credo that I have embraced ever since: "As long as I can identify a majority of stocks that look attractive technically, I'll remain bullish on the overall market."

I came to this conclusion because my work was telling me that this was simply a market that wanted to go up. It was the most powerful thing I had seen in my career — and back then, at age fifty-four with nearly thirty years experience, I was an old man on Wall Street, where the average portfolio manager is thirty and wasn't even around to see the crash of 1987. Few of the thirty-year-olds, or forty-year-olds, or fifty-year-olds understood what was happening.

Once I was convinced of what was happening, the technician in me still screamed out: "Why? What's making this market move higher and faster than any I had seen in over thirty years?"

The answer was that a great many investors were remarkably confident about the future. As we all learned in school, the stock market is a leading economic indicator. That means it moves in anticipation of events. In 1995 the market was telling me — and anyone else who would listen — that we were just entering an extended period of growth. But on the surface, there didn't seem to be any pending news that would cause it to explode upward. I was stumped.

Conventional wisdom on Wall Street says that the market and individual stock prices discount future news events by as much as six months in advance. That's a fancy way of saying that the market and stock prices move long before news is announced. The ability for prices to discount good and bad news is a given. But we now live in an era of heightened public interest in the stock market. Business news has proliferated and is now instantly available to everyone. The tide of data swells bigger every day. Popular TV shows, newspapers, magazines, radio, and the Internet are overflowing with the stuff. This means, I believe, that the normal discounting function in the market has sped up quite a bit. Prices swing more abruptly and more steeply.

But knowing that the market had speeded up, that it was more volatile, didn't tell me what all the optimism was about. Just what was the good news that so many investors seemed to anticipate?

In Catholic school, and in the seminary I attended for two years, I was taught to chase a question until I caught the answer. Baffled by the market, I began to look for historical precedents. A technician must be a market historian. And if the stock market reflects the country and its people, then history probably can help explain events that are out of the ordinary. While individuals are unique, human nature is remarkably consistent. Given the same set of circumstances, we tend to act the same way.

The immediate past didn't help me understand the 1995 market. After the Persian Gulf War rise, the market flattened out and stayed in a very narrow trading range for the next nine months. But now, in 1995, the market was saying that it had no intention of being stuck in idle.

I kept hearing people use the word "unprecedented" to describe what was going on in early 1995, but I knew that couldn't be the case. Almost nothing on Wall Street is unprecedented. In fact, the word should be removed from analysts' dictionaries. Saying something is "unprecedented" is just an excuse for sloppy thinking. I have yet to discover something unique.

So, even though I couldn't initially explain what was going on in the market, I knew there had to be an answer. We must have seen these conditions before. And after a bit of digging, I found that we had. In going back through history, I realized back in the early 1960s, the very market Ken Ward said he found to be the most difficult of his career to call (a conversation I had forgotten about in the intervening thirty years), we had a stock market that kept climbing, despite, as noted before, the Cuban Missile Crisis, the assassination of President John F. Kennedy, and President Johnson's heart attack. That remarkable bull market went on for three years, during which time the Dow gained 75 percent. When you understand that historically stocks "only" increase 11 percent a year on average, you can grasp just how dramatic the gains during the early 1960s were.

So the performance of the market in the early 1960s and the one we were experiencing thirty years later seemed to track fairly closely. And that got me wondering about what else they might have in common.

The answer? Quite a lot.

In the 1960s we had low inflation and a low interest rate environment in the United States. Thinking about what was going on in the market in 1995, I saw that things were remarkably similar. We were at peace in 1995 and we were at peace in the early '60s (Vietnam was just a police action then). In both periods, inflation was low and so were interest rates.

THE EARLY 1960s	MID-1990s
At peace	At peace
Low inflation	Low inflation
Low interest rates	Low interest rates
A booming stock market	A booming stock market

And when I analyzed the market back in the early 1960s, took in all the details, and translated it for the market I was looking at in 1995, the conclusion was clear. We were in another "secular" bull market, one that would last for several years. A typical bull market, for the generation that was used to the 1970s and '80s, doesn't last as long.

In 1995, just about everyone on Wall Street was convinced not only was the run-up over, but that we were headed for a severe bear market.

I thought they were wrong.

I was convinced history was repeating. But, even so, I thought for a very long time before I went public with my conclusions. Hard though it is for all of us — including me — to remember, when I published my research report in June 1995 calling for the Dow to reach 7,000 in less than three years (March 1998 to be exact) the Dow Jones Industrial Average was just at 4,500, and that was following a dramatic run up of nearly 900 points.

I swallowed hard and put my thoughts down on paper. In words that I worried might haunt me for the rest of my professional life, I wrote: "It's now time for the reader to make the critical decision. Are we in the final days of the great 1995 rally or is there much more upside potential left? If you fall into the first camp, then we would recommend cash, now! If you are really bearish and correct, then a meaningful sell-off could happen at any time.

"But we respectfully disagree with the bears. We think we are in one of the greatest bull markets in history. The approach that has worked best for us so far is the bottom-up approach [meaning you look for good stocks, instead of trying to search out macro-indicators]. And it is still working like a charm. In the 1962 to 1966 period, the average group gained 99.8 percent. Today, the average group is up only 21.9 percent—there is quite a bit of room on the upside."

It turns out I was not bullish enough.

PEACE IS BULLISH

How can I explain what has happened since? The current bull market, which I date to beginning in November 1994, is now about six years old and has already advanced roughly 200 percent. We do have a stubbornly strong economy, which the Federal Reserve has begun to address, and it's not clear that they have finished raising rates. This means a bumpy ride for stocks. But the reasons for the mega-market — peace, new technology, optimism, the aging of the baby boomers — have not changed. We have to weather bear markets and understand that while they may slow down the mega-bull, they will not kill it.

You just have to be able to step back and try to find the reasons that explain why mega-markets perform the way they do. I looked back. And what I discovered is the fact there have been three earlier periods in Wall Street's history, periods that I now have named "mega-markets," when the market has behaved similarly.

THE THREE PREVIOUS MEGA-MARKETS

Period	DJIA Gain	Number of years
1877-1891	280 percent*	14
1921-1929	496 percent	8
1949-1966	519 percent	17

*There was no Dow Jones average at that time. This is a gain in what is now known as the Cowles Index.

My research has convinced me that we are right in the middle of the fourth mega-market. I'm defining a mega-market as a bull market that lasts a minimum of eight years and a maximum of seventeen years during which the Dow gains 400–500 percent. If I am right — and all of my research convinces me that I am — then a Dow of at least 20,000 in the foreseeable future is not out of the question.

On the face of it, talking about a Dow that has already doubled doubling again doesn't sound like something a rational person would propose. But if you look at the three previous mega-markets and compare them to what is going on today, you will discover that not only does the prediction make sense, but it is the only possible explanation for the dramatic increase in stock prices that we have experienced over the last six years.

All of the three previous mega-markets had several factors in common. One of the most notable factors is that they each occurred during a peacetime economy, in the immediate aftermath of massive demilitarizing of our armed forces. The first mega-market, the one that occurred between 1877 and 1891, evolved after the Civil War ended in 1865, and soldiers on both sides flowed back to the farms and into the civilian workforce. The rapid expansion out West, fueled in part by the railroads, and increased productivity of the Industrial Revolution kicked our economy — and the stock market — into high gear.

The second mega-market occurred after the end of the First World War and resulted in the aptly named Roaring '20s, when the stock market increased four and a half times in value in the space of just eight years.

The third mega-market began shortly after World War II ended, as America started on its journey to becoming a true economic superpower, fueled by the resources that no longer had to be devoted to the war effort. In the seventeen-year period between 1949 and 1966 the Dow Jones Industrial average climbed 519 percent!

We are now, I believe, in the middle of the fourth mega-market, one that began when we truly understood that the Cold War was finally over. The assets we had once devoted to the military-industrial complex, in order to make sure that we could remain a strategic superpower, are now being reassessed, reduced, and reallocated. To vastly oversimplify, in the midst of the Cold War, when Russia was "the evil empire" and the Berlin Wall was firmly in place, after our best young computer whizzes and engineers completed school they headed off to work for a defense-related company. Today, they are likely to work for — or start — their own software firm, spurring productivity gains and creating new jobs.

All mega-markets evolve because of the following axioms:

War is inflationary.

Peace is deflationary.

War is unproductive.

Peace is productive.

War is a time of fear and despair.

Peace is a time of hope and prosperity.

Gen. William T. Sherman said, "War is hell." I say, "Peace is bullish." The psychology at work is obvious. Each of the mega-markets occurred during a time when the American people felt good about themselves and were recovering from a period of fear and destruction. Peace builds hopes and dreams. And as people feel that their property and their families are safe, they are more willing to spend on new cars, new homes, and, indeed, on stocks. Peace fuels the market in many psychological ways — stimulating investors to buy and causing P/E multiples to expand.

Peace also drives the economy in tangible ways. For every stealth bomber the government cancels, our national economy is about $1 billion richer. That's $1 billion that can be put toward productive use in the economy, instead of being warehoused in an Air Force hangar somewhere. Some of the money that would have been spent entirely on defense is now finding its ways back into the economy, creating new jobs.

Of course, the more people who are working, the more people there are paying taxes. And since the government isn't forced to borrow as much money, the demand for funds lessens, allowing interest rates to slacken, further spurring economic growth.

Each of the four peace-driven mega-markets has also been fueled by explosive growth in technology. Often these technologies grow out of the resurgence of energy, the excitement of free people not diverting their time and efforts pursuing an enemy, and the additional money that need not be spent on the tools of war.

The result in every case has been remarkable transformations in the way we live, work, play, and interact. In the first mega-market, we saw the burgeoning of the oil, railroad, and steel industries. In the second mega-market, it was the widespread introduction of automobiles and trucks. In the third mega-market, it was television and the creation of a national highway system, both of which helped to truly unify the country.

And, in the fourth mega-market, it's another form of highway — the information superhighway called the Internet — and the computerization of our society. Together these forces are as great as, if not greater than, the Industrial Revolution was.

THE PAST AND THE FUTURE

New technologies and peace. They are an almost magical combination. But we cannot underestimate the third element in mega-markets, psychology. When people think tomorrow will be better than today, growth is almost guaranteed. When they do not feel optimistic, growth will grind to a halt. Remember when Richard Nixon was on national television saying "I am not a crook," and later when Jimmy Carter was talking about America suffering through a great "malaise"? No one was optimistic, and the economy was in the doldrums.

Today, most of us are upbeat about our future and our country's peacetime prospects. We are willing to buy stocks at higher price-earnings multiples than we would have paid in the Nixon and Carter years, because we are convinced that we will more than recover whatever premium we pay. That's how people acted in the late 1800s. And in the 1920s. They did it in the 1950s, and they are doing it today.

History repeats. Given the same set of circumstances, most people react the same way each time. The market, too, has patterns and those patterns also repeat. I believe that the technical characteristics of the market since late 1994 have been telling us that we are living at a turning point in the history of our country. But the technical characteristics of the market also make two other things clear:

1. This is not a new paradigm — the rules governing how stocks behave have not been repealed. Trees didn't grow to the sky in the past, and they are not going to start doing that now.

2. We have not entered a new economic era where the traditional rules of supply and demand have been repealed and economic cycles have been eliminated. Both remain firmly in place.

We have to respect these two constants, even while in the midst of a mega-market. Renewed inflationary forces and subsequent interest rate hikes by the Federal Reserve are sure to recur and will definitely slow the market down for a while. These are inevitable events, especially after the first five years of spectacular stock gains. But on a longer term basis, any set-back (bear market) will provide the astute market timing oriented investor with several major buying opportunities.

CHAPTER 2

TECHNICAL ANALYSIS 101

I HAVE BEEN A TECHNICAL ANALYST for more than thirty years and
if there is one thing I've learned over that time it's that most people haven't a clue what I do for a living. They just don't understand
what technical analysis is all about, or they just "get" a small piece
of it and consider themselves an expert.

"I know all about technical analysis," they say, "I can read a
chart," and they ignore everything else. In 1991 the Market
Technicians Association came up with the following definition of
what we do as market professionals. Here it is, in our jargon:
"Technical analysis is the study of data generated by the action of
markets and by the behavior and psychology of market participants
and observers. Such study is usually applied to estimating the proba-
bilities for the future course of prices for a market, investment, or
speculation by interpreting the data in the context of precedent."

The definition I use is a bit simpler. To me, technical analysis is:
"The study of the forces of supply and demand in any free and orderly
marketplace."

As you can see, either definition implies that all forms of investing
or trading — in equities, commodities, options, foreign markets, fixed

income, or currencies — can be analyzed technically. However, since we can't cover everything in one book, we'll focus here on stocks.

I picture stock analysis as being comprised of two parts of the same circle.

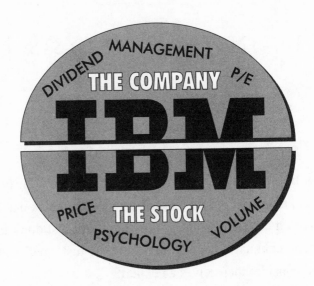

On the top half of the circle is the place where you find the answers to all the questions traditional fundamental analysts ask: How much is the company earning per share? What multiple does it carry? How does it shape up against its competitors in the industry, at home and overseas? What is the strength of its management team? What new products does it have in the pipeline? How is it adapting to changes in technology, etc.?

The top half of the circle represents the way most investors (and most analysts) approach the market. These are the tools used by people who believe in value investing, the approach made famous by the authors Graham and Dodd and popularized by Warren Buffett.

Value investors will tell anyone who will listen the only way to make money is to buy good companies that are being undervalued by the market and hold on to them until their inherent worth is recognized.

But no matter how well they master the fundamentals, those who depend solely on fundamentals are missing half the picture, the technical side that could help them make a more well-rounded assessment and more timely buy/sell decisions. On the bottom half of the circle are the three primary disciplines that comprise technical analysis:

1. Price. Technicians refer to this as "momentum" since the price of a stock is always moving, be it up, down, or sideways (neutral).

2. Volume. This is the number of shares bought and sold, or what technicians also call "the flow of funds." Money is always either flowing into (accumulation) or out of (distribution) a given stock.

3. Psychology. Here we try to determine investor sentiment. Are they feeling positive (bullish) about the stock market overall or pessimistic (bearish)?

The top half of the circle, the fundamentals, tells you what to buy or sell, while the bottom half of the circle, the technicals, tells you when to buy or sell it. Technicians are market timers. We are always trying to determine whether it is the right time to buy or sell a particular investment.

I am not saying that the bottom half of the circle is more important than the top when it comes to analyzing a stock. And much to the chagrin of my friends who do fundamental analysis, I am not saying the top half of the circle is more important than the bottom. What I am saying is that you shouldn't separate the company from its stock price, if you want to determine what it is worth. Just because the fundamentals "prove" that a stock should be trading at $25 a share doesn't mean that it will. You need both halves of the circle to do the job. With both, you can feel pretty confident that you have a solid understanding of not only the company's "fundamental" value, but also whether its stock price will be heading up or down.

THE POINTS OF THE DIAMOND

You may have doubts. I understand. A lot of people I talk to look at the circle image, nod their heads, and promptly dismiss the whole idea of technical analysis out of hand. "Studying the fundamentals has worked for me up until now," they tell me. "And I really don't think I need the bottom half of your circle."

Well, there are some people you just can't get through to, no matter what. And I recognize that. But I am a teacher, and I am determined to try. So for these people, I talk about the importance of technical analysis by using the imagery of a diamond to help make the point.

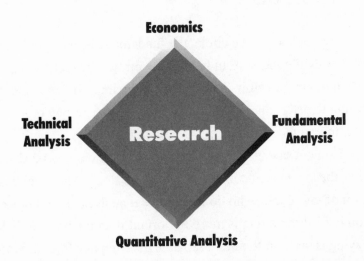

Most people are willing to grant me that the key to selecting quality investments is good research. Since that is the case, they agree that the word "research" belongs at the center of my diamond.

The other points of the diamond include:

- A general sense of the economy. Neither companies nor the stock market operate in a vacuum. Even a company with the best fundamentals in the world is apt to be trading at the lower end of its historic price/earnings range, when interest rates are at 13 percent or higher as they were in the 1980s. At times of high interest rates it's awfully hard to get people to buy stocks — which historically produce an 11 percent annual return — if they can get substantially more than that, with less risk, by buying a Treasury bond backed by the U.S. government. Back in the early 1980s, long-term Treasuries were yielding 17 percent. No wonder the stock market was in the tank back then. To me the point is clear: You have to start with a credible economic overview, along with believable interest rate forecasts.

- Fundamentals. Once you have established your macro economic overview, then you must research the sectors and groups that you think will do best within your economic scenario. And, of course, the next step is to research all of the companies within each group, looking for the best companies with the strongest fundamentals (the top portion of my circle).

- Quantitative analysis. This is work done by people who look at the way the fundamentals have performed over time, and then back-test everything to come up with a model that they think will work going forward. For example, suppose the S&P 500 has a P/E (price/earnings) multiple of twenty-five times earnings and you are wondering whether the stock market is overvalued. A "quant" will start his research by figuring out where the stock market has traditionally traded. (The answer turns out to be somewhere around eighteen times earnings.) Based on this fact, the quant will conclude that stock prices in our example are too high — they are trading at a third more than their normal range — and he will tell people to sell.

- Technical analysis. Most technicians will start out by evaluating market indicators in order to get a sense of what the overall market trend may be. And then, the technicians will most likely separate the stronger from the weaker performing groups relative to the market (S&P 500). Once this task is completed, he or she will most likely scrutinize the price and volume action of each stock within these groups in order to uncover the most attractive and least attractive issues.

You'll notice that I put technical last in this discussion; I did that for a reason. You do all your homework, and then — and only then — you time your decision to buy or sell. With this by way of background, let's talk about how you can use technical analysis to improve your performance.

IN SEARCH OF CONTEXT

I think that we technicians are our own worst enemies. I mean, we work in a field that most people don't understand, and then we seemingly go out of our way to obscure what we do. You can see that in the language we use. We don't say "and people start selling the stock when it reaches 25." Instead, we say there is "resistance" when the stock hits 25. And where the rest of the world says, "The stock looks cheap at 20, and so there are plenty of buyers when it falls that low," we technicians say, "There is support for the stock at $20 a share."

We also make it harder to get our ideas across by presenting our analysis with images that are unusual, to say the least. We use phrases such as "falling flags" and "head and shoulder tops." As a result, even someone trying to accept technical analysis has a hard time understanding it.

The analogy, I suppose, would be if you were sitting in medical school and listening to a description of how the ear works in one class, and then learning all about the Achilles' tendon in the next, and being forced on your own to figure out how all the parts of the body tied together. You could do it, but it would be a lot easier if you were presented with an overall framework to use. That is what I am going to try to do here, give you an overview, which I hope will put in context everything that we will talk about from here on out.

The first option, or point of context, is the macro view. You look at the market from the top down, searching for overall trends, and then you look for stocks that can take advantage of them. I use several macro theories to support my recommendations. I begin with the oldest technical hypothesis of them all: Dow Theory.

Charles Henry Dow, the founder and first editor of *The Wall Street Journal*, created Dow Theory in his search for a better way to understand exactly how well the U.S. economy was doing in the late 1890s.

Dow thought that by monitoring the collective performance of a dozen key firms — mostly industrial — he would be able to tell at a glance how the rest of U.S. companies — and therefore the rest of the American economy — was doing.

Initially his idea didn't work. Dow concluded two things from this experience:

First, he needed another average made up of a different part of the economy, and second, he would have to determine how these two indices would work with each other.

He decided to create his second index around railroads. It became known as the Dow Jones Railroad Average. When asked to explain his decision, Dow said that since the industrial companies make the products this country needs and the rails ship them, together they represent the economy as a whole. He was right, but the indices still needed a bit of tweaking. By 1928, the industrial index had grown to thirty stocks, and the railroad index was increased to twenty, the numbers at which they remain today.

The Dow lists, which are maintained by *The Wall Street Journal,* are changed periodically to make sure they still represent a fair cross-section of the American economy. For example, on January 2, 1970, the *Journal* made a major change. They did away with the old Dow Jones Railroad Average. It became the Dow Jones Transportation Average. They kept the list at twenty companies, but they modernized it by dropping nine railroads and adding companies ranging from airlines to shippers to trucking firms.

The most recent change took place on November 1, 1999, when the *Journal* changed the Dow Industrials to help reflect today's new economy. They removed Sears Roebuck, Goodyear Tire & Rubber, Chevron, and Union Carbide. They added SBC Communications (one of the "Baby Bells"), Home Depot, Microsoft, and Intel. These last two are the first non – New York Stock Exchange listed companies ever to appear in the Dow Jones Industrial Average. Both are found on NASDAQ. (It is interesting to note that only General Electric remains from the original Dow list. GE has always been a highly adaptive company, changing to fit markets, and this probably explains its longevity atop the U.S. economy.)

Despite the changes — or probably because the changes have been made to reflect the ever-evolving nature of our economy — the Dow continues to be an accurate tool.

Ironically, Dow himself never wrote out his underlying theory in its entirety. That task was done by S. A. Nelson in a book entitled *The ABC of Stock Speculation.* William P. Hamilton, the second editor of the *Journal,* wrote about it frequently; and Robert Rhea explained Dow's ideas in *Dow Theory Applied to Business and Banking,* a long-forgotten book which was published in 1938.

Both Nelson and Rhea explained that Charles Dow started with the premise that everything we know about a stock is reflected in its price.

That is an extremely powerful idea, one that has been studied by all technicians. Let's spend a minute on why such a simple statement is so important.

Think about what the share price represents. What we think is the intrinsic worth of the company is there, of course. That's what the people who believe in the fundamentals study. What the market thinks about the company's earnings per share, sales growth rate, and position within the industry is also reflected in what the stock is trading for.

But the share price reveals much more. It reflects how we feel about the economy, the political environment, interest rates, you name it; it's all there in the share price.

Having doubts? Well, think about what happens when people are worried about rising interest rates and inflation. Stock prices fall — maybe a lot, maybe a little — but the fact is that they decline. As we said before, when we are uncertain about our political leaders, prices fall. And if we are expecting a recession? Prices fall again.

The converse is also true, of course.

Think about what happens when people are feeling good about the economy, the country's future, and/or their own circumstances? Prices rise.

The most fundamental thing about a company is the price of its stock. It is the most important input that we have.

After considering price, Dow took it a step further. He reasoned that if you look at the price changes in both the Industrial and Railroad indices, you will have a good understanding about how everyone feels about the economy as a whole both today and tomorrow. As those indices move, buyers and sellers are telling you with their money how they feel about the entire U.S. economy.

As Rhea put it: "The closing prices of the Dow Jones Rail and Industrial Averages offered a composite index of all the hopes, disappointments, and knowledge of everyone who knows anything of financial matters, and for that reason the effects of coming events (excluding acts of God) are always properly anticipated in their movement."

The intriguing thing about Dow Theory is that it requires both the Dow Industrials and what is now the Dow Transports. Both averages must break through previous important overhead resistance levels to prove a bullish trend. When both of the Dow's averages are making new closing highs — and Dow thought the close was the most important price of the day — the stock market is said to be in a primary bull market. Conversely, if both averages are scoring new closing lows, then we are in a primary bear market.

It sounds simple enough, and it is. But remember, stocks don't move in a straight line. They zig and zag, and they may fall significantly during an up move and rise a great deal during an overall decline. Dow understood this, and so he took great pains to explain what we should look for in charting the performance of both averages. He identified three key movements.

The most important is the primary trend. This is exactly as it sounds. It's the overall direction of a market or stock during a given time. It is possible, Dow wrote, that a primary trend could last five years or more.

The second, and most deceptive, movement is the secondary reaction. Dow defined this as an important decline in a primary bull market, or a rally in what is otherwise a bear market. These secondary reactions, he said, "are likely to retrace from 1/3 to 2/3 of the preceding primary swing." That isn't as difficult to understand as it sounds. All it means is if the Dow Jones Industrial Average has gone from 10,000 to 11,000 during an up move, it is more than possible that it can fall back as low as 10,333.33 — giving back two-thirds of its gains — without the primary trend being over.

Conversely, a market that fell from 12,000 to 10,000, could bounce back to as high as 11,333.33 — a climb of two-thirds off the low — and still be in a decline.

The third, and least important, movement is the daily fluctuation. Stocks, Dow understood, jump all over the place on a daily basis, a fact that did not concern him greatly. He was looking for the over-arching themes. Now that you understand what the Dow Industrial and Transportation indices tell us, it is fairly easy to understand how a technician puts Dow Theory into practice.

SHIFT FROM A PRIMARY BEAR TO A PRIMARY BULL MARKET

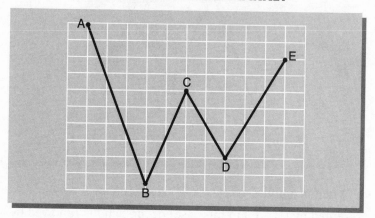

As Rhea explains, "in every bear market (A – B) there always comes a time when a rally develops." This rally (B – C) is the secondary reaction that we talked about above. The rally may stall and turn back down (C – D), but if it doesn't make a new low (below point B), technicians start to smile.

Why?

Because Dow Theory is telling us that a potential shift in the market's primary trend is in the making. We may be heading from bearish to bullish. For that to be the case, "the subsequent advance (D – E) lifts prices above the secondary high point previously established (C)," Rhea tells us. That is what is exactly going on in the chart on the previous page. "With volume increasing on rallies, and contracting on declines, the primary trend, according to Dow's Theory, has changed from bear to bull."

Dow Theory also predicts bearish moves.

SHIFT FROM A PRIMARY BULL TO A PRIMARY BEAR MARKET

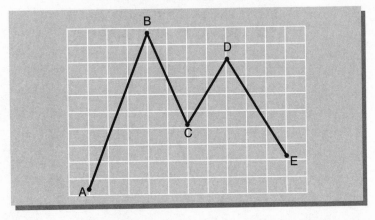

"When in a bull market (A – B), a secondary reaction [the decline represented by (B – C) in this case] occurs, and is followed by a rally (C – D) that approaches, but does not better the previous high point (B), and then if a later decline (D – E) forces the prices of both Dow averages below the preceding secondary low point (C), the primary, or long term trend, is considered to have changed from bull to bear."

Rhea used a nice ocean image as a way of keeping all of this straight. He suggested that we think of the three movements — the primary trend, the secondary reaction, and the daily fluctuations —

as being the tide, the wave, and the ripple, all acting, reacting, and interacting at the same time.

To play this analogy out, we would consider a bull market as the rising tide and a bear market as a tide that is falling, always remembering that regardless of whether the tide is ebbing or flowing, a) they are both tides, and b) those tides will be interrupted by waves rushing in and then receding. Remember, these waves, secondary reactions, are temporary. They do not prevent the tide from either rising or falling completely.

How do we know when we have moved beyond wave action and the market is about to change direction? Rhea continues his ocean imagery to provide the answer.

Suppose that you are walking on the beach and are curious about whether the tide is rising or falling. You could watch the waves, and push a stick into the sand at the highest point the water reaches. If you need to keep moving the stick up the beach, the tide is rising. If successive waves fall farther down the slope away from the stick, the tide is going out. And so it is with the averages. If after many days, the averages keep registering higher prices, you are in a bull market. If, day after day, the prices recede, you are facing the bear.

SUMMING UP DOW THEORY

Charles Dow sold his interest in Dow Jones & Co. in 1900 to Clarence Barron, and very little is known about him after this time. Still, his legacy remains. With periodic changes to the averages, Dow's theory remains as relevant today as it was one hundred years ago. It is one of my key inputs. I need it because my primary job is to identify the market's major long-term trend, and Dow Theory is remarkably good at doing just that. I guess my loyalty to the Dow averages makes me a traditionalist when it comes to technical analysis. I start with the basics and continue to use a series of basic technical tools throughout my research efforts.

MARKET PSYCHOLOGY

Another important element is market psychology. Bernard Baruch said: "What actually registers in the stock market's fluctuations are not the events themselves, but the human reactions to those events. The stock market is people . . . their hopes and fears, strengths and weaknesses, greed and ideals."

No doubt, Baruch read about investor psychology in Dow's writings in *The Wall Street Journal*.

THE PSYCHOLOGY OF A BULL MARKET

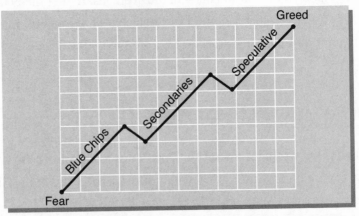

Dow understood the emotions behind most investment decisions. Investors fear losses, gain confidence when profits start to flow, and ultimately succumb to greed. In the beginning of a bull market, fear dominates because the pain of the previous bear market is still fresh in the minds of investors. Thus, when these skittish buyers come back to the equity market, they will be tentative and more apt to buy conservative stocks. They will look for stocks with a history of solid earnings and those that traditionally have had a secure dividend.

This tentativeness explains why a classic bull market starts with a run-up in the prices of blue chip stocks. But as a bull market progresses and investors become more confident, they are very likely to change their equity mix. They become more willing to take bigger risks. At some point leadership will shift away from the conservative issues (now that these formerly nervous investors consider those stocks to be boring blue chips) and move toward secondary stocks.

These secondary issues will provide new and more exciting stories, and equally important, since investors still have some memory of the last bear market lingering in their brains, they will appear fundamentally more attractive. They will be good values. This is the second phase of a classic bull market.

As surely as night follows day, the lure of rising stock prices will attract more and more buyers. These new participants are less likely to know what they are doing and more likely to demand unreasonable returns. The types of stocks bought during this, the third and final phase of a bull market, can only be described as speculative. The name of the stock will be as important as what the company actually earns or what it does.

By the time a market enters the third stage we have reached the point where greed rules the mind and the bubble will burst. This is how the second mega-market ended, with the Crash of 1929. All mega-markets do end. However, we are a long way from this point in the current mega-market. And there are invariably large, flashing warning signs, from a technical point of view, that will allow you to get out in time. We will be talking more about this later in the book.

THE PSYCHOLOGY OF A
BEAR MARKET—THE 3 Cs

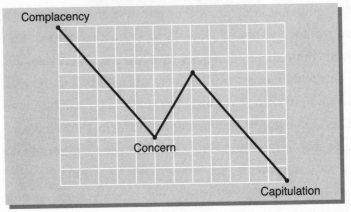

People new to the Street often think they've invented this kind of analysis. But Charlie Dow laid it all out for us a century ago. Just as he described the three emotional cycles of a bull market, he also identified the three emotional themes of a classic bear market: complacency, concern, and capitulation.

The beginning of the typical bear market starts at the very end of the latest bull market. Investors at this point are overly confident, even arrogant. They'll buy just about anything, convinced that this time trees will grow to the sky. They are fat, dumb, and happy, or in Dow's word, complacent.

When the bear starts making itself felt, and the "buy on the dips" philosophy doesn't work anymore, investor losses start piling up. At this point, complacency quickly turns to concern. Their new battle cry? "I'll sell during the next rally."

Well, you guessed it, the next rally either doesn't materialize, or it isn't strong enough or doesn't last long enough to satisfy them. In either case, they fail to liquidate their losing positions. Now they are really stuck with all the dogs they bought. They worry as they watch the market grind lower and lower every day.

Once the pain level gets so high that they are losing sleep at night and dealing with margin calls during the day, these scared "investors" capitulate. "Get me out at any price!" they scream. And the bear market reaches the "selling climax" stage.

Eventually, though, people regain their footing and take their first tentative steps back into the market — buying blue chips — and the cycle starts all over again.

As I said before, individuals are unique, but collectively human nature remains the same. Charlie Dow understood this and technicians should too.

TIME CYCLES

My good friends and fellow technical analysts at Yelton Fiscal have provided me with a useful introduction to time cycles. Before the modern-day business cycle was developed, most economic times were marked by crises — wars, plagues, famines, or even high levels of speculation such as the tulip mania in the seventeenth century when speculators bid the price of bulbs to astronomical levels.

But as economies matured and people began to take notice of rhythms in the business process itself, patterns were spotted and the study of "business cycles" as a tool to measure activity was born. Hundreds of studies have been done on the subject of cycles. Here we will only touch on a few before spending more time on a cycle that I have found to be remarkably reliable.

In 1860, Clemant Juglar published his book *Des Crises Commerciales et Leure Retours Periodique en France, en Angleterre, et aux Etats Unis.* In sum, his book concluded that the economies of England, France, and the United States went through regular economic cycles; periods of expansion would be followed by contraction, and so on and so on.

Juglar used interest rates, stock prices, banking statistics, and commodity prices to come up with what worked out to be a pattern that repeated itself every 9.25 years. This has since become known on Wall Street as the decennial pattern. It is interesting to note that if stock prices are random, there can be no cyclic patterns. Yet this 9.25-year cycle has been repeated sixteen times since 1834. The odds of that happening at random are more than 5,000 to 1.

Others have identified amazingly accurate patterns in the economy. In 1923, Professor W. L. Crum of Harvard published the results of his examination of commercial paper rates from 1866 to 1922. He found a forty-month cycle that could be observed with remarkable regularity.

At the same time, another Harvard professor, Joseph Kitchin, found cyclical patterns on wholesale prices, bank clearing, and interest rates in the United States and England during the period he studied, 1890 to 1922. This four-year cycle — known as the Kitchin cycle— has held pretty firmly from 1950 to today.

Another Harvard economist, Joseph Schumpeter, has authored a two-volume work called *Business Cycles: A Theoretical and Statistical Analysis of the Capitalist Process*. Schumpeter's theory was that innovation was the father of economic expansion and that depression was the adjustment to the excesses that are part and parcel of any boom period. He combined the cycles of Juglar and Kitchin and others to devise a complex system that can be used to follow the economic tides.

As you can see on the Summation Cycle graph opposite, the last time all the time cycles bottomed together was in the late 1940s, early in the third mega-market. They are turning up together again as I write this.

My favorite time cycle is the presidential election cycle. State and local elections, except in very special cases, have little or no impact on the stock market. However, presidential elections are quite another story. There is an uncanny relationship between presidential election cycles and what happens in the stock market.

THE SUMMATION CYCLE

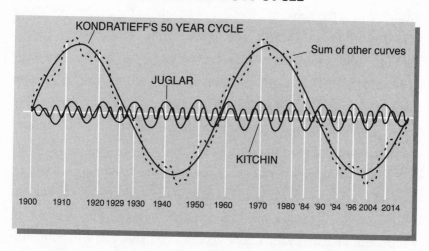

At first this relationship may seem odd. But it is not. Think about what you would say if your party had just won the election and you were advising the President of the United States of America.

I would advise my commander-in-chief to do all the "tough things" early in his administration. That might mean doing some very unpopular things such as raising taxes, freezing social security benefits, etc. Getting these politically difficult decisions out of the way early increases the odds that the president will have enough time to make moves that will please people as it comes time for him to run for a second term, or in the case of a second-term president for him to set up his chosen successor.

"Just imagine all the new tax cuts and increases in old age benefits that you can propose just before the next election campaign starts," I'd tell the president. "They would be a real popularity boost."

It seems I am not alone in my thinking. Look at how Wall Street has typically reacted during each term of a new administration — Republican or Democrat. Historically, Wall Street greets new presidents from either party with a "honeymoon rally." Investors are either glad that the old party is out of power or thrilled that the policies of the previous administration are going to be continued. They are more than willing to give the new president every benefit of the doubt; that's why there has traditionally been a rally following the presidential election.

This rally could carry into the second year of the four-year term in office. But sometime during the second year, a market correction (or even a bear market) commences. This could be the result of those unpopular decisions discussed before. The ending of this decline will most likely coincide with a four year low. The market's tendency to bottom out every four years is absolutely amazing.

The president's third year in office is usually the best year out of all four for the stock market, possibly because this is when an administration usually announces economic plans that will help with the reelection. Remember, Wall Street is a discounter. It moves in anticipation of events. So, even though that economic stimulus might not take place until the president's fourth year in office, the markets will respond immediately to the fact that good times are coming. The last year of an administration, the election year, is usually an up year for the stock market as well.

MAJOR MARKET BOTTOMS HAVE BEEN RECORDED EVERY FOUR YEARS

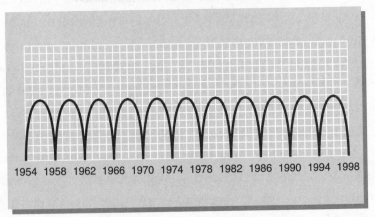

1954 1958 1962 1966 1970 1974 1978 1982 1986 1990 1994 1998

Why does this cycle always hold? Because presidents, like all politicians, want to win votes. Investors vote. So, by passing along some positive pieces of legislation the president increases his odds at the polls in the coming election. Likewise, investing according to presidential cycles has proved remarkably rewarding.

FINAL THOUGHTS

This is just a taste of technical analysis. By incorporating these technical theories and many more into my research, I am able to create a top-down outlook for the overall stock market. This helps give me a macro (long-term) view of Wall Street. And as I said earlier, you have to have a long-term market opinion. Without it, you will not be able to trade and/or invest properly. Without it you will use your technical tools incorrectly.

In the next chapter, we'll move from the macro to the micro to learn how to use correctly the technical tools for picking individual stocks. This will be of most interest to those who want to learn about chart reading; others might want to skip ahead to Chapter 4.

CHAPTER 3

HOW TO READ CHARTS

No MATTER WHICH SET of statistics technicians accumulate and research, they first plot the numbers on charts. Charts are an invaluable tool when it comes to deciding where you should put your money. The reason is simple. In investing, just as in life, the past is prologue. If you know what happened before in a specific set of circumstances, you will have a pretty good idea what might happen in the future, should those circumstances come around again. A chart, as the critics of technical analysis love to say, is just history. And my response: You can learn an awful lot from history. We are a collection of all of our past experiences and in order to better judge the future you definitely need to understand the past.

Technical analysis, which relies heavily on charts and graphs as a means of discovering recurring events (noticeable price and volume patterns), is particularly important now because the market has been telling us since late 1994 that we are living in a time of great change. But what we are going through now, we have experienced before. Charts help you understand this and profit from that understanding.

AN INTRODUCTION TO CHARTING

Charts come in four varieties: line, bar, candlestick, and point and figure graphs.

Let's go over all of them quickly, to give you a passing familiarity with what they are, before spending the most time on bar charts, the charting technique that is most frequently used in the United States.

Line Charts. This is where you simply plot and connect closing prices of a stock or a market average over a fixed period of time: daily, weekly, monthly, or annually.

A SIMPLE LINE CHART

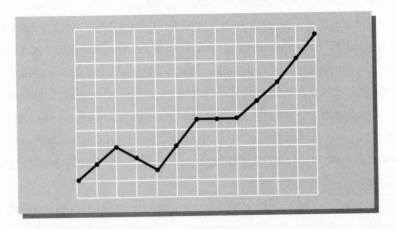

As you can see in the chart above, while plotting the price over time, the line chart gives you a good indication of direction: where price has come from and where it might be headed.

BAR CHART:
PRICE AND VOLUME

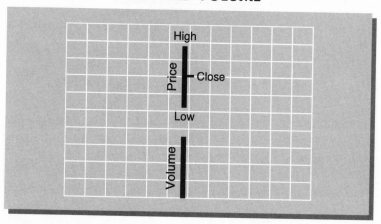

Bar Charts. This kind of chart records the high, the low, and the closing price on a daily, weekly, or monthly basis. And now with the advent of computerized real-time prices, anyone who is a very aggressive day trader can easily capture the high and the low of price on a minute-by-minute basis. Note how the volume bar is placed directly beneath the corresponding price bar.

MINUTE/MINUTE BAR CHART
Intel Corp.

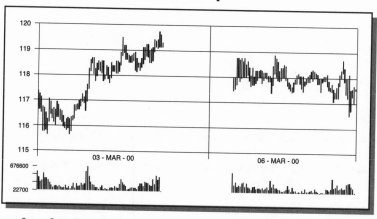

Source: Bridge Information Systems

DAILY BAR CHART
Intel Corp.

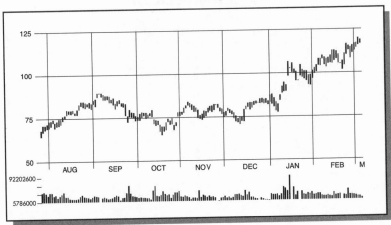

Source: Bridge Information Systems

WEEKLY BAR CHART
Intel Corp.

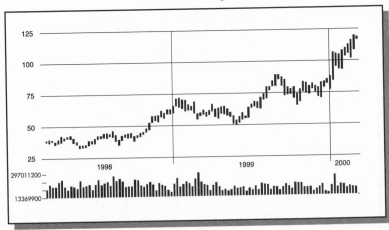

Source: Bridge Information Systems

MONTHLY BAR CHART
Intel Corp.

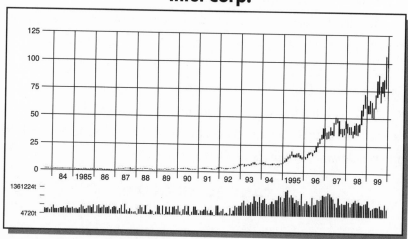

Source: Bridge Information Systems

Let me point out something that I am sure you have already noticed. The physical size of all of these bar charts is the same. But, because of the different dimensions for each price and volume bar, the time span covered on each graph varies dramatically.

The following table shows you what I mean.

TYPE OF HISTORY SEEN ON THE MOST COMMONLY USED CHARTS	
Minute/minute	One full day to three days
Daily	Usually 6 months/sometimes 1 year
Weekly	Usually 2 years/but sometimes up to 5 years
Monthly	Usually 10 years/but sometimes up to 20 years

Now, let me make an important point. When it comes to charting, one size does not fit all. Each type of chart is designed for a different type of investor, and you have to use the one that's right for you, if you are hoping to increase your chances of success.

Candlestick Charts. I am sure you noticed that when I began talking about bar charts earlier I stated that it was "the charting technique most frequently used in the United States." I made this statement because technical analysis isn't just an American phenomenon, its history dates back many years and crosses into other parts of the world including Great Britain and Japan. The Japanese are having an impact on technical analysis in our country today. And the man most responsible for this is an old friend of mine, Steve Nison, who in 1991 authored *Japanese Candlestick Charting Techniques*.

CANDLESTICK CHART:
PRICE AND VOLUME

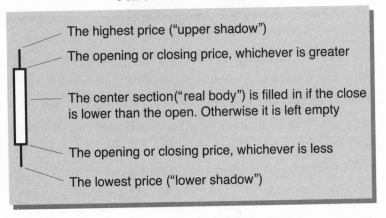

The highest price ("upper shadow")

The opening or closing price, whichever is greater

The center section("real body") is filled in if the close is lower than the open. Otherwise it is left empty

The opening or closing price, whichever is less

The lowest price ("lower shadow")

Candlestick charts actually give you more information than regular bar charts and should definitely be incorporated into your technical studies. Read Steve's book for greater detail on this subject, but in the meantime I will provide you with a brief insight into how these charts are constructed and how best to use them along with the other three varieties of charts.

Unlike the data used in bar charting, candlestick charts include the opening price, along with the high, low, and close plus volume. It is the fact that it shows the relationship between the stock's opening price and its close that makes this variety of charting unique.

The combination of empty bars (positive activity) and filled-in bars (negative activity) gives the user a better feel of supply and demand as price patterns emerge. These bars can also be plotted on a minute-by-minute, daily, weekly, or monthly basis. Hence, just like the bar charts mentioned earlier, candlestick charts can be used for aggressive day trading all the way up to and including long-term investing.

Point and Figure Graphs. This is the oldest form of charting in the United States. It dates back to Charles H. Dow, who recorded stock prices (literally, the figures); he called this the "book method" or "figure charts." These figure charts record each sequential one-point move — up or down — in a stock's price. You keep marking new prices in one column until there is a reversal of one full point; then you switch to the next column to the right. You stay in the new column and mark increments of one full point until there is another reversal of one full point; then you switch to the right again.

DOW'S ORIGINAL FIGURE CHART

30	30			30					
29	29	29	29		29	29			
28	28		28	28	28	28	28	28		28
27		27	27		27	27	27	27		27
26		26	26	26			26	26	26	26
25		25	25					25	25	

Sometime in the late 1890s a man by the name of Victor de Villiers adjusted Dow's charts by replacing the figures (except for grid numbers) with Xs; hence the name, as we know it today, point and figure.

A POINT & FIGURE VERSION
OF DOW'S FIGURE CHART

30	0		0			0				
	X	X	X	X		X	X			
	X	X		X	X	X	X	X	X		X
	X			X	X	X	X	X	X	X		X
	X			X	X	X		X	X	X	X
25	5			5	5			5	5	

There are two schools of thought on the construction of point and figure charts — the Wheelan Method and the Abe Cohen Approach. Wheelan uses *intra-day price reversals* to record a basic one unit chart. It the same graphing technique used by Dow and de Villiers and shown above.

The followers of the Cohen approach use *intra-day highs and lows* but only make marks on the chart to reflect reversals when there is a reversal of three points or more. The result is a chart with less "noise" but also less detail.

COHEN'S THREE-POINT
REVERSAL CHART

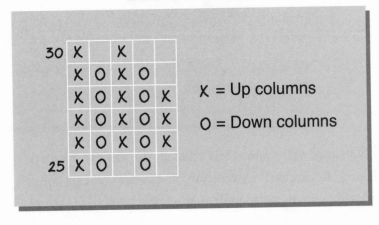

X = Up columns

O = Down columns

I am a big believer in and user of point and figure charts. However, they do not record volume nor do they really capture the element of time as precisely as bar and candlestick charts do. But having said all of this, I believe that one of the biggest advantages in using point and figure graphs is their ability to project intermediate and long-term targets. Bar and candlestick charts are unable to do this as well as point and figure charts.

USE THE RIGHT TOOL

When you wake up in the morning, you have to ask yourself, "What am I?" If your answer is, "I'm a day trader," you'll want to be looking at how a stock — or the market overall — is trading tick by tick. For you, long term is between the opening bell and lunchtime.

But if you are planning to be in the market on a longer term basis — say you are investing for a goal that is at least six to ten months out — what do you care if the stock you are following fell a quarter of a point in the last hour, in the last day, or even in the last week? You are interested in the bigger picture.

If your time horizon falls somewhere in between, you are a traditional trader. You are thinking about holding a stock for a few days to a few weeks.

No matter what your investment horizon is, it is very important for you to understand who you are and how long you are planning to hold a specific stock. Only then can you select the chart that is appropriate for what you are trying to achieve.

I am almost embarrassed to dwell on this. Yet I consistently find day traders looking at long-term charts, and people who are investing for the long haul looking at technical information that is best suited for day traders.

And it isn't just individual investors who are making these kinds of basic mistakes. I find professionals making the same mistakes. You can't do that. You have to use the chart that is right for you.

I know that this may sound ridiculously obvious, but the fact is that an enormous number of people don't use the right charts. They are ignorant (or maybe it's arrogant) and assume that a chart is a chart. As a result, they end up making very expensive errors. I want to make sure that you don't.

Is one kind of chart better than another? Is it better to look at short-term charts, as opposed to monthlies? Does one set of charts give you more accurate information than another? The answer to all of these questions is no. All charts are equally valid, and in fact I look at all of them all the time. I have to. I'll get a phone call in the morning from one of our financial advisors asking what I think stock X will do between now and early afternoon, and a couple of minutes later someone might stop into my office to ask how that same stock is likely to perform over the next twelve months.

Both the day trading chart I looked at in the morning and the long-term chart I study in the afternoon can give you accurate information. You just have to know what kind of investor you are. The answer will dictate precisely which chart you should use because, as we have seen, there are different tools (charts) for different objectives.

The following table may help keep it all straight.

WHAT IS THE RIGHT CHART FOR YOU TO USE?		
Type of Holding	**Appropriate Activity**	**Period Chart**
Day trading	Less than a day	Minute/Minute Bar and/or Candlestick
Traditional trading	Days to weeks	Daily Bar and/or Candlestick. One Unit Point & Figure (Wheelan)

Type of Holding	Appropriate Activity	Period Chart
Intermediate term	Six to ten months	Weekly Bar and/or Candlestick. Three-Point Reversal Chart (Cohen)
Long-term investing	At least one year	Monthly Bar and/or Candlestick. Three-Point Reversal Chart (Cohen)

HOW TO READ A CHART: EYES RIGHT

After years of teaching the basic course in technical analysis at the New York Institute of Finance, I can honestly say that I know how to help take the mystery out of reading charts. My students tell me they find that comforting, and I can understand why. I know that charts can be overwhelming, confusing, and even intimidating when you look at them for the first time. I tell all of my students that regardless of what type of chart they use, and no matter how confusing it may appear at first blush, the very first thing they must do is to place their eyes correctly upon the graph.

Always start with the most recent price and volume activity — and that is always found on the extreme right side of the chart.

Then place your left hand over the graph, exposing about two inches of the most recent price and volume activity, which is on the right side of the chart.

Once you have done this — and with your left hand still covering three quarters of the chart — get under way by asking yourself the following questions.

RALPH'S FOUR QUESTIONS:
- What are the stock's minor and major trends? (Which way is the stock's price moving?)

- Where is the support level? (At what price do investors find the stock attractive enough to buy?)
- Where is the resistance level? (At what price are people willing to sell?)
- What upside or downside objectives are there, if any? (Realistically, how far up, or down, can we expect the price of the stock to go?)

After answering these questions, drag your hand farther to the left, exposing about half of the chart. Again, ask yourself those same four questions.

- What are the stock's minor (short term) and major (long term) trends?
- Where are the potential buyers (support levels)?
- Where are the potential sellers (resistance levels)?
- What upside or downside objectives are there, if any, when it comes to the stock's price?

After you have completed this exercise, lift your hand from the chart and examine the entire graph. Yes, ask yourself Ralph's Four Questions once again. Now let me offer you some guidance in your effort to answer the questions.

What is the trend?

We are talking about the stock price here, and I don't want to sound too simplistic, but prices can only do one of three things: prices can go up, they can go down, or they can move laterally (stay in a neutral trend). And yes, they will gyrate all over the place, but the fact is that within the specific time frame of the chart you are using you will always be able to discover a trend that is moving either up, down, or sideways.

To find it, simply go through your three choices systematically. Are we in an uptrend? Uptrends occur when the stock makes a series of higher lows and higher highs in price.

UPTREND IN PRICE

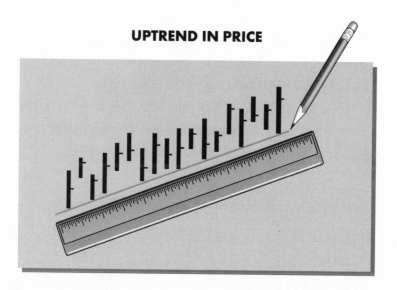

How do you find out if you are in an uptrend? Take a ruler and pencil and draw a line connecting the ascending lows. As long as the price bars remain above your newly drawn trend line, as it does in the above chart, the stock is in an uptrend, or, as some people like to say, it has an upward bias.

Are we in a downtrend? That is a situation that occurs when the stock's price registers a series of lower highs and lower lows.

DOWN TREND IN PRICE

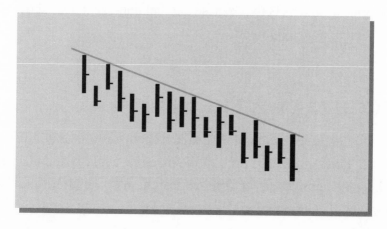

To find out, draw another trend line (see previous page). This time you are connecting the descending highs. As long as the price bar stays below your trend line, the stock is said to be in a negative trend. It can also be described as having a downward bias.

Are we in a neutral trend? The only other choice is for the stock to be in a flat or neutral trend, a situation where charting the price reveals that there are a series of parallel highs and lows in price.

NEUTRAL TREND IN PRICE

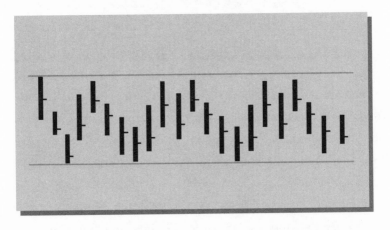

To find out if you are tracing a neutral trend, connect the highs with a line and then draw another parallel line that tracks the lows. If the price meanders between these parallel lines, as it does above, you have a flat, or neutral trend.

ACCURACY IS THE KEY

So far, I hope, everything I have talked about has been easy to understand. This is the way I present the material in class, and occasionally someone will say, "Come on, Ralph, get on with it. This is all obvious." I always respond the same way.

"It is obvious, but it is vitally important. You have to have the basics of charting down cold because even the smallest error can throw everything out the window."

For example, I can't stress enough the importance of drawing correct trend lines. It seems so easy and so simple to draw these lines, but somehow many technicians either get sloppy or simply forget the definitions. As a result, they often mislabel price trends or draw them in where they simply don't belong.

MINOR AND MAJOR TRENDS ARE UP

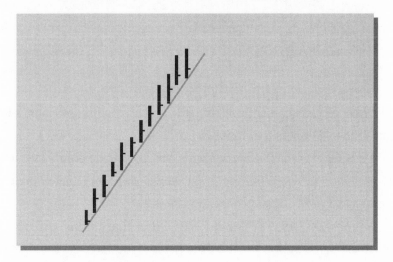

For example, the chart above shows a simple uptrend. The chart on the next page, however, depicts a stock price that is moving laterally away from the original uptrend line.

The question? What is the chart on the next page revealing to us? To find our answer, we return to the basics. Remember, you begin your interpretation of any chart by turning your eyes to the far right side of the graph, using your left hand to cover most of the chart, so that only a small portion of the most recent price activity on the extreme right side of the chart is visible.

THE UPTREND WAS BROKEN,
IT IS NO LONGER IN FORCE

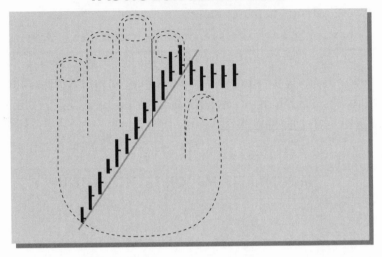

Now, as you stare at the chart ask yourself the first of Ralph's Four Questions: "What is the minor trend?"

I suspect you will agree with me that the most recent price activity reveals a series of parallel highs and lows. Since that is the case, your answer is: "The minor trend is neutral."

When you lift your hand from the chart, you will expose all of the price action for the time period you have selected. When you lift your hand, you'll notice that the previous major trend was up — but that this uptrend is no longer in force — therefore, your answer to the question "What is the major trend?" will also be neutral.

In the next graph, shown at the top of the next page, I purposely drew in an incorrect uptrend. This second trend line is wrong because the most recent price bar(s) never reestablished new, higher lows and higher highs after penetrating the first uptrend line. The correct uptrend example is seen below it on the next page.

THE SECOND TREND LINE IS INCORRECT

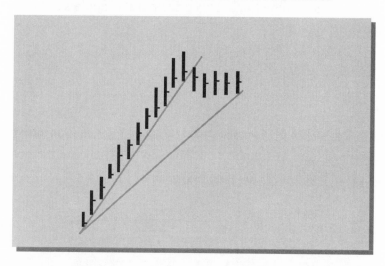

THE SECOND UPTREND IS CORRECTLY DRAWN-IN

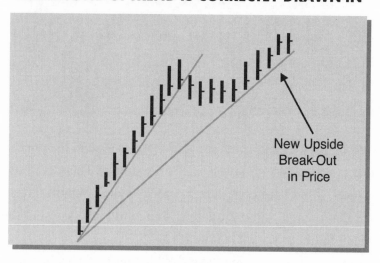

New Upside
Break-Out
in Price

Note the new upside break-out in price. Now a new set of higher lows and higher highs are in place. Therefore, you can draw in the new (second) uptrend line, which would confirm the fact that the stock is heading higher. We technicians would also say that this stock is experiencing the "fanning principle," which is, by definition, a series of broken trend lines. This principle also applies to downtrend lines.

Where are the potential buyers, and where are the potential sellers?

Let us now examine a neutral trend. Doing so will help us answer the second and third of Ralph's Four Questions: Where are the potential buyers, and where are the potential sellers?

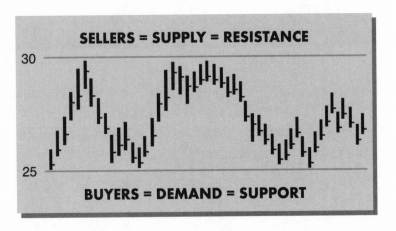

Note that every time the stock dropped to around the price of $25 a share, it wouldn't go lower. Why? It's simple. There are buyers at this level. If there weren't, then the stock would fall until it reached a price that people found attractive. You could also say that there is demand for the stock when it trades at 25.

Conversely, every time the stock hit a high of 30 you notice that it was unable to move higher. Again, the explanation is quite simple. There are more sellers at 30 than buyers; if there weren't, then the stock would move higher. You could also say that there is too much supply of stock for sale coming at 30.

It is too bad that the words "support" and "resistance" crept into the technicians' vocabulary. The problem isn't the words themselves, it's that too few were ever taught to connect these two words with the more commonly accepted words, "buyers" and "sellers."

"Support" means an area of demand. It is the price at which people are willing to buy.

"Resistance" is a area of supply. It's the level at which people are willing to sell.

It all ties back to my simplified definition of technical analysis: "The study of the forces of supply and demand in any free and orderly market."

THE PERCEPTION OF CHANGE

My primary objective as a technician is to identify the major trend. Once I have accomplished this task, the second most important part of my job is to identify when that trend has changed. Like a navigator, my responsibility is to plot the course and to inform the pilot (the owner of a stock) whenever I detect that the airplane (the stock) is off course.

A simple trend violation is one way to determine whether there is a significant change in the direction of the stock's price. In other words, it is often a way to determine if the plane's course needs adjusting.

When is a deviation from an upward trend line important?

There is no one quick answer to this question because everyone's risk tolerance level is different. In the case of an uptrend, a mere intraday breach of this trend line might be enough of a violation for a very aggressive day trader to sell his entire position.

THE PENETRATION OF AN UPTREND

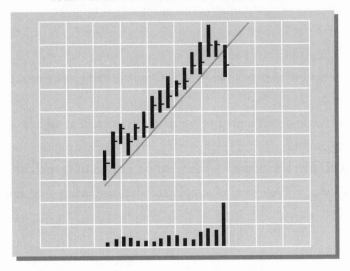

On the other hand, a longer term investor might insist that price must close below the uptrend line — by at least 3 percent on a 50 percent increase in the stock's average daily volume — before conceding that the trend is over.

These strict criteria are obviously not for everyone. And let me stress that I am not advocating that you incorporate this particular set of rigid disciplines into your approach to the markets. Everyone is different and has a different level of risk he or she is comfortable with. But you need to establish some set of "risk management rules." That way when a shift occurs that meets your criteria of when a trend is sufficiently broken, you'll have enough warning about this loss of upside momentum so that you will be able to minimize your risks.

Everyone wonders "What should I look for that will be a sure tip off that a stock could be heading higher?" I'll tell you again that the answer will depend on how aggressive you are. But I can tell you that when an important downtrend is broken by a upward move in price of at least one full closing point on heavy volume you should start rethinking your negative outlook on this particular stock.

*What upside or downside objectives are there,
if any?*

Answering this question is a much more complex endeavor but one that, if done correctly, should be very profitable. In order for this to make sense, I need to explain how prices can theoretically change or move over time. For lack of a better name, I am going to call this the Four Phases of Price Activity.

FOUR PHASES OF PRICE ACTIVITY

You can't buy or sell volume nor can you accumulate or distribute investor sentiment (the psychology component that we talked about earlier). At the end of the trading day, your fortune is always measured by how well your stock price has fared.

So let us investigate what the theoretical path of price is other than just a simple up and down motion, based upon the diagram on which all of technical analysis is built: the Four Phases of Price Activity.

THE FOUR PHASES OF PRICE ACTIVITY

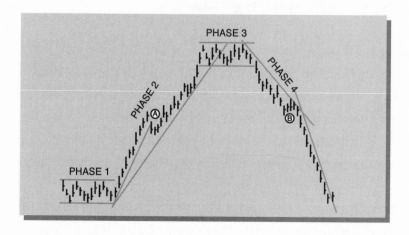

Phase I. The price is in a pronounced neutral trend. It is moving within a relatively narrow trading range. As time passes, a keen-eyed technician, using a combination of price patterns, volume formulas, and momentum indicators, notices that the shares are being accumulated. The stock price still hasn't moved much, but more and more buyers are coming in. We technicians call this situation "the base-building phase." It is clear that the stock is "bottoming out," that is, we can say with some certainty that it is not going to head any lower. (A quantitative analyst might describe the company as a value stock, because the share price is depressed and it appears that the market has discounted all of its negative fundamentals.) The technical price patterns that form during this phase are called major reversal patterns. They indicate that the stock's next major move will be to the upside.

Phase II. The stock price is clearly in a major uptrend. The quants would describe the company we are diagramming as a "momentum stock." There are times when the stock will undergo normal profit taking (A), but even so, new buyers rush in and eventually carry the stock higher. The price formations that occur throughout this uptrend or mark-up phase are called continuation patterns, suggesting that this stock has further upside potential.

Phase III. Price reverts from a strong upward bias back into a pronounced neutral trend. Initially, the stock is consolidating recent gains, but as time passes, signs of distribution emerge. The sellers are more dominant than the buyers. Technically, the stock is topping out. The price patterns that form during this phase are called major reversal patterns. The quants would say that this stock is overvalued.

Phase IV. Here price breaks down from its topping formation and enters a major downtrend. There are times (B) when the stock will stop going lower. It will consolidate for a while at a given level, but over time it comes under renewed selling pressure and continues to fall. The price formations that materialize during this downtrend or mark-down phase are called continuation patterns, suggesting that this stock is vulnerable to falling even further.

Now that you have a basic understanding of the Four Phases of Price Activity, I hope that you will always stop and ask yourself the following questions before you buy or sell:

- Is my stock bottoming out (in phase 1) or topping out (in phase 3)?
- Is it too early to buy, because the stock is still heading lower (in phase 4)?
- Is it too early to sell, because it is still heading higher (in phase 2)?

Your answer will save you considerable anxiety in the future. (And, by the way, congratulations. Just by asking them, you have become an official market timer.)

Now, let's briefly touch on three tools — moving averages, Advance/Decline Lines, and relative group performance — that we can overlay upon the Four Phases of Price Activity.

A TREND-FOLLOWING TOOL: MOVING AVERAGES

Earlier in this chapter I discussed how to draw trend lines manually on your chart. I also said that far too often some technicians tend to draw those trend lines incorrectly.

In order to remove subjectivity from the trend lines they draw, technicians have devised moving averages (MA), which are basically nothing more than mathematical trend lines. When incorporated on charts, moving averages can be extremely helpful. They are very simple to construct.

Take, for example, the most popular version we use: the 200-day moving average. The moving average is exactly what it sounds like. You add up the closing prices of a stock — or a market average such as the Dow Jones Industrials — for 200 consecutive trading days, then divide by 200 to get the average of the past 200 days.

It is called "moving" because the average does indeed change over time. On day number 201, the first day is dropped, the closing price for day 201 is added, and you divide by 200 once again.

THE FOUR PHASES OF PRICE ACTIVITY PLUS MOVING AVERAGES

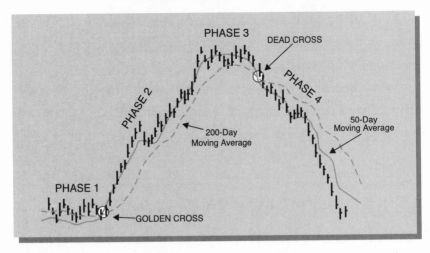

Once you overlay the moving average upon the Four Phases of Price Activity as we do above, you will notice that the MA trails the actual price. This would make sense because the moving average includes the last 200 trading days, and the net effect is it smooths out all the daily price volatility. The main thing to keep in mind here is that as long as the price of the stock you are charting remains above the 200-day moving average, the stock is most likely enjoying positive price momentum. Once the stock price crosses below its moving average, as it does here, it is said to be losing price momentum and apt to suffer continued weakness.

The 200-day moving average is a trending tool that is very helpful in confirming the existence of bull and bear markets as well as major up and down trends for individual stocks. Obviously, it is of a relatively long-term nature. (After all, 200 trading days is equal to about ten months of data.)

If you have a shorter term orientation, you could use a 50-day moving average, which works exactly the same way, but just uses fifty trading days of data. This is more useful to those who are intermediate-term oriented (about ten weeks of data). And of course you can fine tune the moving average to last just five or ten minutes, if you so desire.

What time frame you use depends on your objectives. The rules still apply no matter what. The price must stay above the moving average for the trend to be considered valid and in force.

I encourage the simultaneous use of moving averages (for example, a 50-day and a 200-day); this should help lessen the false signals you get when price activity whip-saws above and below one moving average. When the shorter term moving average (the 50-day) crosses above the longer term one (the 200-day), it affords a major buy signal, known in Japan as the "Golden Cross." Theoretically, you continue holding this stock until the reverse happens — the 50-day crosses below the 200-day. Our technical friends in Great Britain refer to this second pattern as a "Dead Cross," a major sell signal that stays in force until you see another golden cross.

MARKET PARTICIPATION—
THE ADVANCE/DECLINE LINE

In the 1930s a man by the name of Colonel Leonard P. Ayers believed that one could gain a vision of coming business events by counting the number of steel plant kilns in full operation. His observations went even further. He counted things such as the number of stocks that advance versus the number that decline every day on the stock exchange. This provided, he felt, an instructional picture. He was very correct. His count was the forerunner of what we technicians now call the Advance/Decline Line (A/D Line). This is one of our basic indicators. It helps us identify in what direction the majority of stocks are headed, what technicians call the breadth of the market. If more stocks go up than go down during a certain period of time, breadth is described as positive. More losers than winners? Breadth is negative.

The Advance/Decline Line is remarkably easy to figure out. On any given day some stocks will go up, some will go down, and others will remain unchanged. You simply subtract those that went down from those that went up, ignoring those that were unchanged.

To get an overall sense of the market's breadth, technicians accumulate the net difference between those stocks that advance versus those issues that decline every day. The A/D Line will give you an indication of how broad-based a market's rally or decline really is.

I wanted to give you a brief history of this important and very basic tool because it is causing quite a stir these days. The New York Stock Exchange A/D Line peaked in July 1998 and hasn't exceeded this high since. During the same period of time the Dow Jones Industrial exceeded its 1998 high and has gone dramatically higher.

In technical parlance this is called "negative divergence." When the majority of stocks (the A/D Line) fail to confirm the strength of the leading blue chip stocks, the Dow Jones Industrial Average, the market's leadership is said to be too narrow and so the market's uptrend is not said to be sustainable.

THE FOUR PHASES OF PRICE ACTIVITY
PLUS THE ADVANCE/DECLINE LINE

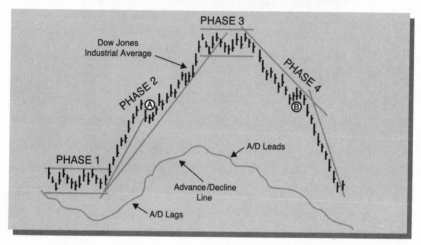

Ordinarily, three to six months of negative breadth — that is three to six months where there are more losers than winners when you plot the Advance/Decline Line — results in some kind of market sell-off or correction. Most of us in the technical fraternity accept this A/D correlation as a given. Note in the above theoretical diagram that the A/D Line lags in the early stages of an up move versus the DJIA because blue chip stocks (quality) rise first.

Similarly, the Advance/Decline Line leads at market tops because traditionally the deterioration of the overall market begins with the bulk of the stocks moving lower despite the strength in the quality names. The big winners (leaders) are the last to go down as we enter a bear market.

The accepted wisdom is that the stock market cannot keep going higher when there is a long stretch of negative breadth.

But I don't think the accepted wisdom applies to the current market. Unlike today's long-term bearish technicians, I am not calling for the end of this current bull market just because the Advance/Decline Line is in a multiyear downtrend. Yes, I know that's what I am supposed to say. But my research has convinced me that this time is the exception to the rule.

When you read the following chapters, you will discover that long-term negative breadth is actually normal during mega-markets. A negative Advance/Decline Line is part of the fabric, it's inherent in the DNA, if you will, of a mega-bull market.

GROUP AND STOCK LEADERSHIP

I love the old adage: "It is not a stock market but rather a market of stocks." This statement is one of Wall Street's best truisms. And yet almost no one believes it. Test it out. Ask a couple of individual investors, "What did the market do today?" I'll bet most will respond in terms of the Dow Jones Industrial Average. They say the Dow was up forty, or down twenty, or whatever it happened to do. They won't mention the performance of the Russell 2000 or the Wilshire 5000; for sure most won't tell you how many stocks advanced versus the number that declined that day.

The public thinks that the market is the Dow. Unfortunately, they are wrong — the stock market is a composite of many stocks (about 3,000 issues on the NYSE). But the fact that they are wrong doesn't matter. That's how they think, and how they think influences how stocks will perform. That's why you have to be familiar with how the Dow Jones Industrial is performing.

The "pros" on the other hand, pay more attention to the Standard & Poor's 500. For portfolio managers, the people who run mutual funds, pension funds, hedge funds, etc., the S&P 500 is the market. Their charged responsibility is to "beat the market." They must outperform the market (the S&P 500) in order to get their bonus or (if they fail to do so on a consistent basis) keep their jobs.

The best tool to help uncover groups and stocks that are outperforming and/or underperforming the market is comparative relative strength. It is a simple calculation: The closing price of the stock divided by the closing price of the Standard & Poor's 500 equals comparative relative strength. Plot the comparative relative strength line below the stock's price bar.

If the comparative relative strength line is going up that means that the stock is outperforming the market (S&P 500); if the comparative relative strength line is going down that means that the stock is underperforming the market (S&P 500). And lastly, if the comparative relative strength line is flat (neutral trend) that means that the stock is even with the market (S&P 500). There are only nine possible combinations of price versus the comparative relative strength line.

There are really only four out of these nine combinations that you want in your portfolio because the others will, over time, hurt your overall performance. The four are: uptrend in price with uptrend in relative strength; uptrend in price with neutral relative performance; neutral price with uptrend in relative performance; and, neutral price with neutral relative strength.

If you scrutinize stock charts with the intent of owning only those stocks having one of the four characteristics listed above, then you will have a portfolio of stocks doing at least as well as the market, if not doing a lot better than the market. Yes, the charts can truly help if you only take the time to look at the most important aspects — and comparative relative strength is one of these.

NINE COMBINATIONS OF ACTUAL PRICE AND RELATIVE STRENGTH ACTIVITY

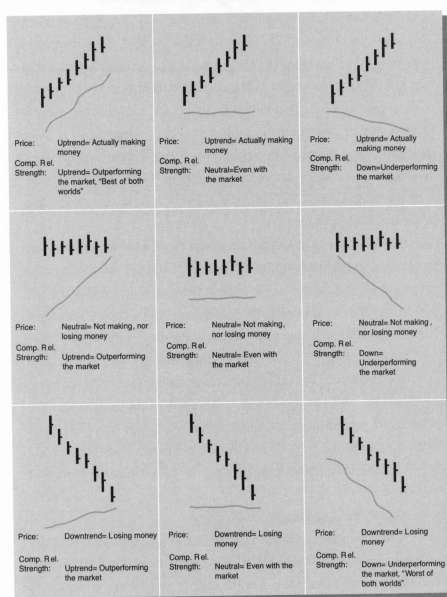

Price: Uptrend= Actually making money

Comp. Rel.
Strength: Uptrend= Outperforming the market, "Best of both worlds"

Price: Uptrend= Actually making money

Comp. Rel.
Strength: Neutral=Even with the market

Price: Uptrend= Actually making money

Comp. Rel.
Strength: Down=Underperforming the market

Price: Neutral= Not making, nor losing money

Comp. Rel.
Strength: Uptrend= Outperforming the market

Price: Neutral= Not making, nor losing money

Comp. Rel.
Strength: Neutral= Even with the market

Price: Neutral= Not making, nor losing money

Comp. Rel.
Strength: Down= Underperforming the market

Price: Downtrend= Losing money

Comp. Rel.
Strength: Uptrend= Outperforming the market

Price: Downtrend= Losing money

Comp. Rel.
Strength: Neutral= Even with the market

Price: Downtrend= Losing money

Comp. Rel.
Strength: Down= Underperforming the market, "Worst of both worlds"

SUMMARY

For many people, technical analysis is unfamiliar territory. So let's spend a couple of pages reviewing all the things I touched on in the last two chapters.

It's always best to start with the macro approach. How's the market doing? And I mean all aspects of the market — starting with the Dow Industrials (blue chips) and going all the way down to the S&P Small Capitalization Index (secondary stocks). Make sure that you study the NASDAQ Composite — this is a quick way to view technology stocks.

You want to go through a three-step process:
- First, identify the major trends for key market averages.
- Then isolate the best relative performing groups.
- And finally, pick the technically attractive stocks within these better acting groups.

When you are looking at the market the other way — and remember we talked about the importance of looking at the market, in the words of Joni Mitchell, from "both sides now" — you take a different tack.

For your micro, or bottom-up approach, where you start with analyzing stocks and then build to an overall take on the market, you want to:

- Identify your goals and objectives.
- Select the proper chart(s) that will aid in attaining your goals.
- Start analyzing that chart by staring at the right side of the chart first.
- Then answer Ralph's Four Questions.
- And finally, determine where your stock fits in with the Four Phases of Price Activity.

If you do all of this, your ability to not only select stocks but also determine when to buy and sell them should improve.

Here's an example of how this functions in the real world. When I was a young analyst, I got a call from the manager of a large portfolio. His boss had given him a project: He was supposed to research AT&T and Eastman Kodak and decide by the end of the day which was the most attractive for long-term purchase. After serious research he concluded that both companies were excellent long-term buys; however, he could only select one. He called all the fundamental analysts he knew. They all liked both of them. It was three minutes before the closing bell and the guy was desperate. Then he called me.

Realizing he was a long-term investor I immediately grabbed my weekly and monthly bar charts. I knew that both stocks were selling at the same price. But I saw in the charts that AT&T was in phase two ($60 in an uptrend) and Eastman Kodak was in phase four ($60 but in a downtrend) of the Four Phases of Price Activity. The choice was obvious, and he made it.

We can follow the same process to assess the market overall. By studying the major trends of the leading averages you can determine what phase the market is in. By looking at these trends and comparing this market to previous mega-markets I'll show you why I believe the current mega-market is in phase two of the Four Phases of Price Activity and will ultimately continue to go up.

CHAPTER 4

THE FIRST MEGA-MARKET: 1877–1891

I FELL IN LOVE WITH HISTORY as a boy growing up in the Bronx in the years after World War II. The energy, excitement, and pride were all around me, so it makes sense that I would be caught up. It was, as Studs Terkel called it, "The Good War." I could feel the tide of history, long before I understood its lessons about people, countries, and markets.

When I was older I grew past the flag-waving stage and began to grasp the complexities of war, especially its destructive evil. Much of war flows out of greed and hatred, and it is, at its base, a reflection of human failure and ultimately failed politics. But this does not diminish its central role in human history. Countries and continents have been shaped by war. So, too, have the very identities of many peoples. For proof you need not look any further than the recent conflicts in the former Yugoslavia. The Serbs, Croats, and Bosnians have existed for centuries in an atmosphere poisoned by war. Each group formed a culture of mistrust that was just waiting to explode in the 1990s.

Besides shaping peoples and societies, modern war has also had a dramatic effect on technology. Ironically, the inventions and infrastructure created for war — roads, explosives, iron-clad ships, radar — have always been turned to peaceful uses that make life better. In America, this occurred in a dramatic way after the Civil War, when railroads, steel, the telegraph, and oil transformed life.

These innovations, and the remarkable American spirit, ultimately created the first mega-market, which began in the late 1870s and ran up to the early 1890s. Unfortunately, data about this period is sketchy, especially compared with today, when we have an endless number of indices and minute-by-minute charting available. But some numbers are available, and we can look at the stories of individuals and industries to get a sense of what happened. There is no doubt that a mega-market occurred in this time, and I believe it was stimulated in large part by the innovations of war and the powerful conditions created by a protracted period of peace.

To understand the dramatic impact of this mega-market, to fully grasp the change it created in everyday life as well as in the course of the nation, you have to look first at life just prior to the war. It was, in many ways, the same way of life that had existed for a hundred years or more.

LIFE BEFORE THE WAR

In 1860, fewer than 31 million people called themselves Americans. We were not yet a nation of immigrants. In fact, only 4 million were foreign born. A boy born into a typical American family of the time would be the descendant of immigrants from Northern Europe. Though New York, Boston, and Philadelphia were major cities, he lived where the majority of people lived — on a farm or in a small town. Imagine a farm outside a small town in western Massachusetts.

Our Pittsfield boy didn't look forward to much mobility, either economic or geographic. Most of the adults he knew were born, lived, and died without venturing more than a few miles from town. They eked out a living on family farms or in the village. Back-breaking labor was normal for the working man. Keeping a home required all of a woman's energy, and our little boy would have been put to work in the fields or his father's shop by age six or seven. If he was lucky, he would receive a few years of formal education.

In the cities of 1860, American industry had begun to grow, but it was slow to develop and concentrated in a few types of manufacturing. To be realistic, the country had just one major industry — textiles. Almost every other manufactured good for sale was made somewhere else. There was no oil industry to speak of, and the same could be said for steel. And if there were any major industrial leaders, they were not substantial enough to be remembered today. Indeed, in 1860 the number of millionaires in all the country could be counted on two hands.

This doesn't mean that progress was stalled. The great technological development of the time was the railroad, and tracks were being laid to connect major cities. But no line yet linked the East with the West. And where service existed, it was expensive, inconvenient, and inefficient. Just one train per day served to connect Washington, D.C., and Boston, for example, and with all the switching from one carrier to another — along with trips on ferries — the journey required days of discomfort.

If you are picturing America as a second-rate economy exporting mainly raw goods — cotton was the big one — you are mostly right. America was poor, compared with much of Europe, and its economy was just beginning to awaken.

Politically, the country was bitterly divided by slavery and other issues of "states' rights." In this crisis, almost nothing else mattered. Southern politicians were talking secession and ordinary citizens worried about the possibility of war and a divided nation. Families expected that fathers and sons would become soldiers, and they knew that many of them would be killed or wounded.

WAR AND PEACE

The horrors of the War Between the States have been told, in their tragic complexity, by countless historians. The invention of the Gatling gun, and the wide use of artillery, meant that the American Civil War was the first modern war, complete with all the carnage that suggests. Battlefields literally turned red as new weapons and tactics made it possible to kills thousands of men in a matter of minutes. At Cold Harbor, Virginia, 7,000 died in twenty minutes. This was unprecedented.

Despite the human tragedy taking place on the battlefield, the war was an economic boon to the North. Indeed, the Civil War marked the first time when America's economy, from top to bottom, was revved to the point of overheating by government spending.

The war effort required enormous increases in output from farms, mines, and the forests. These formed the backbone of what could be called the Old Economy of the time. But the war also pushed the development of new kinds of enterprise. The raw materials produced in rural areas were processed in new factories to become goods — uniforms, foodstuffs, arms — for the military. Railroads were expanded to deliver men and matériel, and the telegraph network grew to aid communications. At the same time, the North dramatically increased exports to Europe.

In the capital markets, this was good news, especially for the stocks of the railroad companies. Traffic increased dramatically, which meant equally dramatic increases in profit. Between 1862 and 1864, railroad stocks more than doubled in value. (Though records are scarce, this is documented in the Macauley Railroad Index, the best measure of the sector's health.) Other transportation firms enjoyed similar increases in the value of their stocks. Shipbuilders, canal companies, and all their suppliers benefited.

THE MACAULEY RAILROAD INDEX
1857–1875

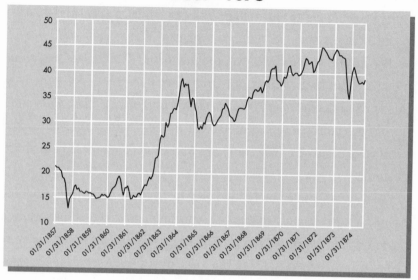

Outside the transportation sector, manufacturers found that the war stimulated inventive genius. Sewing machines were first put into wide-scale use to make uniforms. They transformed the clothing industry and drove prices steadily downward. Other industries benefited from the growing use of steam power, which was far more efficient and flexible than previous power sources like river water.

Of course, the enormous new factories built to supply the war effort needed workers. Young people flocked to manufacturing centers like New York. The cities responded by building housing, streets, water systems, sewage systems, telegraph services, and public transportation. Though Southern demagogues had said the loss of trade with the South would kill the economy and "make grass grow on the streets of New York," the opposite was true. Business boomed.

If you just look at economic numbers — stock prices, exports, mergers, and acquisitions — America seemed ready for an enormous expansion at the end of the war. But psychology plays a key role in markets. All the activity in manufacturing, shipping, and public infrastructure was stimulated by the emergency conditions of the war. When the war was over, people had a chance to catch their breath, and actually consider the human price that had been paid. It was shocking.

By the end of the Civil War, roughly 620,000 men had died either in battle, from their wounds, or from illness acquired along the way. This is more deaths than America suffered in all her other wars combined. Few families were untouched. In the South, entire cities and towns were destroyed. The survivors who made it home told nightmarish stories.

In the years immediately following the war, the American economy should have been ready to race. New technologies, new transportation systems, and growing urban centers all suggested a bright future. We were ready for the first mega-market. But much of business seemed to get stuck at the starting gate. The Macauley Railroad Index reflected this, dropping roughly 20 percent from its wartime high, and staying there.

An easy explanation for the stagnation might be seen in the government's shift to a peacetime budget. No longer required to fund an enormous war, the federal government reduced its spending from $1.3 billion per year at the height of the war to less than $600 million. Still, this figure was ten times the federal budget of the prewar years, so it does not explain the doldrums in the overall economy. That requires an analysis of the national spirit. Deep psychology was at work here.

I believe that at the end of the war the country must have felt both relief and exhaustion. Nations are like individual people. They can be healthy or sick, strong or weak, optimistic or depressed. In the aftermath of the Civil War, when hundreds of thousands of maimed men came back to their families, America was like someone who had gone through surgery and barely survived.

People who have had a serious illness usually feel blessed to be alive, but they are also traumatized. For a certain period of time they may be in shock. When that recedes, they may be afraid the illness will come back. It may take years for them to regain physical strength, confidence, energy, and creativity. Probably the last thing they recover is ambition. Ambition requires both hope and faith in the future.

PROMONTORY SUMMIT

History is real people and real events. And like most trends in history, each mega-market can be traced to a symbolic starting point, a human triumph that heralds the remarkable period of growth to come. In 1869, just such an event occurred. It was so epochal that it quickly became clouded in myth and misstatements. But the clouds cannot obscure its importance.

The date was May 10. The place was Promontory Summit, Utah. (Not Promontory Point, which lies thirty miles to the South.) Two rough and rowdy track-laying crews, one working from the West, the other from the East, met at a predetermined point. A somewhat boozy, frock-coated group of dignitaries gathered to watch as the last spike — iron, not gold — was hammer-driven through steel and wood, completing the transcontinental railroad. The news was sent West and East, by telegraph. In San Francisco, a fifteen-inch cannon was wired so that a telegraph signal made it fire the moment the last spike was driven. On that signal, all the church bells in the city were rung. Street celebrations there went on for days.

The building of this railroad was a stunning display of organization, engineering, and finance. But it was also the work of extraordinary men. (As I've said, the histories of nations and markets are the stories of real people.) The route for the railroad was worked out by engineer Theodore Judah, who plotted a line through the Sierra of California along the same path as the ill-fated Donner party. His daring design was the key to the road's completion, and it has stood the test of time.

Judah was a figure who symbolized the time in which he lived. He was raised in the small town of Troy, New York, where early railroads created a hub. Like today's young people who dive into software development, he entered the growth business of his time, railroading. He proved himself early and rose quickly. By the early 1860s, he was the main engineering proponent behind the transcontinental project. His lobbying in Washington, along with his trailblazing, made the project possible. Though he died before the railroad was completed, his zeal set an example for the men who followed.

The laborers who built the transcontinental railroad, 25,000 in all, were led by teams of foremen and managers, many of whom were veterans of the Civil War. Chief among them was Gen. Grenville Dodge, who had served with Sherman in the Union cause. Dodge turned the track-laying into a military-style effort and employed many war veterans in the cause. The personal discipline, sense of camaraderie, and ability to work in a team — all acquired in the war — were readily converted to peacetime effort. Also valuable was their experience with the tools and technology of war. Having manned cannons, they were unafraid of dynamite.

From the moment the nation was joined together at Promontory Summit until 1879 a full $1 billion (in current dollars this would be about $20 billion) would be spent to expand railroads across the United States. In the same time period, two additional industries — oil and steel — would burst onto the scene as powerhouses of the mega-market. A new kind of history-shaping figure — the Captain of Industry — would be recognized, and the American economy would soar to global leadership.

Of course, none of this was predicted, even amid the celebrations of May 10, 1869. But if you understand mega-markets, you can see that it was inevitable. All the preconditions were in place. Peace had finally been accepted and embraced by the nation. New technologies were poised to transform the way people lived. And the leadership was emerging to make it happen.

VISIONARIES

The great figures of the first mega-market — J. P. Morgan, Andrew Carnegie, John D. Rockefeller, and others — played in an arena where there were almost no rules because most of the regulatory agencies and restrictions we know today had not been developed. Because of this, it would be disingenuous for me to ignore the scandals linked to their excesses. History records the speculation that ruined many small railroads, manipulations of the market, the abuse of labor, and the political scandals. Indeed, one of the great legacies of the first mega-market was the series of corrections made by Congress and the courts, which created a safer, fairer business environment.

Though the turbulence that followed the Captains of Industry was dramatic, I'm concerned more with the ways their personalities, intelligence, and character built and grew the mega-market. They were all, in their own ways, visionaries. They could see great opportunities and moved to exploit them. As early as 1865, Morgan went to Europe to tell investors and bankers that magnificent opportunities were at hand. "We are going to some day show ourselves to be the richest country in the world," he told them.

Morgan was the first great American financier and he built his empire on the New Economy of his time. But as in all mega-markets, he had to ride out many corrections and reversals. His interest in railroads is a good example. In the boom years of railroad construction, competition was fierce. Small lines were built everywhere, but small-scale operations were highly inefficient. Cargo and passengers had to be transferred from one carrier to the next, and many firms were so overleveraged that they never turned a profit.

An investor who followed the new industry but doubted its strength would have found plenty of reasons to turn away as every few months some small rail line went belly up. Everyone talked about bringing some rational order to the system, but no one seemed up to the task. Heck, railroad companies couldn't even agree on how wide the tracks should be.

But Morgan and others recognized the true value of the new technology and stayed in the game. They also sensed, even if they didn't recognize it consciously, that all the factors that determine a mega-market were in place:

Peace

Low inflation

Low interest rates

New Technology

Morgan was there with the financing as the strongest railroads became stronger through acquisitions and mergers. Swallowing up the unprofitable lines, the most ambitious railroaders stitched together ever-bigger route systems, which allowed them to carry passengers and freight for longer distances. The gains in efficiency were obvious, and the general trend in rail stocks was very strong. Morgan rode this trend, handling stock and bond issues for the likes of the Northern Pacific, the New York Central, the Reading, and Pennsylvania.

In a time when many other investors failed, Morgan built an unprecedented fortune by understanding, in his own way, the answers to the four key questions about a mega-market. He understood the major trends in railroad stocks, which were all positive.

What were the improvements? There were two major ones. The first was the introduction of steel rails, to replace iron. The steel rails could bear more weight, were easier to use in construction, and lasted six to eight times longer than iron. The second improvement was in the power of locomotives. During the first mega-market, the power of locomotives increased 100 percent.

It wasn't just the trains that got better. Everything that railroads needed — switches, signals, railroad cars — was being constantly improved and made less expensive. The huge demand for these products made improvements possible, as suppliers competed for ever-bigger contracts.

This explains why the real "infrastructure play" for an investor in the first mega-market would have been in railroad equipment stocks, not the railroads themselves. For example, at the height of the war the Rogers Locomotive and Machine Works of Paterson, N.J., was the most profitable heavy manufacturer in the country. Rogers turned out an astounding twelve engines per month and employed 1,000 men. After all, the railroads were taking enormous risks, building expensive lines without a guarantee that they could beat the competition and ultimately profit. Their suppliers, however, sold their locomotives, steel, and other devices to all comers.

This is why during the first mega-market, railroad equipment stocks rose 850 percent, while the railroads themselves climbed 290 percent. Sounds like the phenomenon that is taking place today. Those companies that are supplying (servicing) the Internet industries are, in many ways, doing better than the Internet companies themselves. Is history repeating itself? I say yes! What we are seeing today happened well over 100 years ago.

THE STOCK MARKET AS A WHOLE

The Cowles Index of stocks, a measure equivalent to today's Dow, shows a bull market for the period, with an overall increase of 281 percent. Like all bull markets, it was not a straight line up. Out of a total of fifteen years, ten were up years with an average gain of 16.5 and five were down years, with an average loss of 6.7. Cowles' best year was 1879: up 50.2 percent. Its worst was 1884: down 13.5.

After the Civil War had ended in April 1865, the Cowles Index (All Stocks) enjoyed an irregularly trending higher market for the next several years. But, as later history bears out, there is usually a post-war stock market decline. This rally/decline scenario ended in 1877 with a Cowles low that was practically back to its Civil War peace-low of 1865. A kind of double bottom, as we technicians would call it.

For the next fourteen and a half years — between its June 1877 low and its December 1891 peak — the Cowles Index enjoyed a gain of about 280 percent. Note, however, that after the first four "up" years (1877 to 1881), the Cowles actually went flat to down for the next four years (1881 to 1885) before moving irregularly higher. Hence, the first mega-market, like all the ones that follow, was not a straight ascent; there were years of lackluster performance. This is normal activity as the mega-market works its way higher.

Statistics on the following nine sectors were compiled by the Cowles people and cover the entire period between 1877 to 1891:

Sectors	Percent Gain or Loss
Coal	+ 205
Industrials	+ 293
Mining & Smelting Misc.	− 57
Miscellaneous	+ 296
Railroads	+ 290
Rail Equipment	+ 850
Shipping and Shipbuilding	+ 200
Utilities	+ 333
Utilities, Telephone & Telegraph	+ 479

Obviously, anyone who invested in the overall market would have realized healthy returns. But those who recognized that there was a mega-market within the Cowles Index would have been able to get out of Old Economy stocks and into just the right New Economy issues to beat the averages several times over.

COWLES' ALL STOCK INDEX
1876–1891

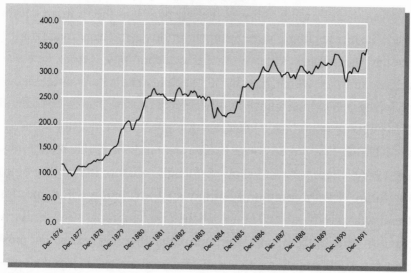

Among the Old Economy stocks, the miners and smelters were the worst. They actually lost more than half their value — 57 percent — as steel and the pressures of competition pushed them downward. No other sector was similarly devastated. However, coal suffered as oil came into production. And shipping and shipbuilding lost out to the ever-growing, ever-faster trains.

The New Economy, mega-market businesses that set the Cowles Index on fire were almost all directly involved in the most exciting technologies of their time. I've already mentioned the rail equipment sector, which increased the most, but there is an interesting aside to this story. Not all of the equipment that made the railroads run was high-tech for its time. One of the most powerful companies in the early 1870s was a shovel-making company in Massachusetts owned by a man named Oakes Ames. Ames and his brother Oliver became so powerful that, for a time, they were major stockholders in the Union Pacific and played central roles in financing the transcontinental line. Ames, who also served in Congress, would eventually be ruined when it was revealed that he sold stock to senators and representatives at cut-rate prices. (I never said the movers of the mega-markets were all innocents.)

As raucous and exciting as the railroads and the railroad equipment businesses might have been, enormous gains were made during the first mega-market in two other new technology sectors. One was electric utilities, which grew by 333 percent. The other was telephone and telegraph, which enjoyed a 479 percent run-up. The forces behind these figures should have been easy for any shrewd investor to recognize. Utilities delivered power to cities and industries that were growing every single year and showed no signs of stopping well out into the future. Every community of any size was being wired and this trend would only grow. The telephone and telegraph were similarly vital to growth. Companies and individuals with access to the most immediate information and communication always enjoyed a competitive advantage. In a very short time this technology became a necessity.

Industrial capitalists, led by J. P. Morgan, were at the center of the development of the electric utilities that sprang up during the first mega-market. Unlike other businesses, the electric companies started basically from scratch. With no real revenues, they relied heavily on bond issues and the sale of stock to raise capital. If you want a comparison, think of the dominant Internet service provider of our day, America Online. Though as of this moment in the year 2000, AOL is a strong profit-making concern, for most of the 1990s it was a net loser and depended on financing to expand.

While he had many choices among the pioneers in electricity, Morgan went with the biggest name and brightest mind, Thomas Edison. In 1878, thirty-one-year-old Edison's invention of a cheap lightbulb, which ran on low power, promised to bring electric light indoors. At the time, homes and buildings were lit mainly by kerosene, gas, or candles. Within weeks of Edison's discovery, the value of Old Economy gas company stocks plummeted 50 percent.

When Edison formed a company to deliver light to the masses, Morgan was there to both purchase stock himself and arrange the sale of more. (Morgan did this despite the vehement opposition of his much-revered father, who thought the new technology was a worthless fad.) Edison would have to move fast. As with any new business, competition arose as soon as the technology was known. And setbacks were many. But every time Edison ran into a problem, and the value of his company dipped, Morgan increased his investments.

This history places Morgan, an investor, at the center of Edison's revolutionary enterprise. Some people, probably most, understand

Edison's genius as an inventor. Others may dimly recall Morgan as a man from the seemingly arcane world of finance. But in fact, Edison would not have been able to invent and develop his electric system without the capital that Morgan either contributed directly or raised. Morgan did all this because he had confidence in Edison's ideas and faith in him as a man.

By 1881, Morgan's faith began to pay off. Edison's display of electricity at an exposition in Paris was a sensation. Soon Edison built a central power plant in New York City with a generator named Jumbo. Edison Electric went on to become a dynamo of this business. Just as successful were independent companies formed in Edison's name to make lights and other electric devices. By the close of the decade, Morgan was there when Edison Electric was consolidated into one large concern. Morgan's investment house came out of the deal holding more than 15 percent of the stock.

Electric companies of the time were faced with the same competitive problems as railroads. It was impractical for separate generating facilities and electric cable systems to be built side-by-side. To be efficient, the utilities needed large numbers of customers within exclusive service areas. Inevitably, consolidations occurred. In 1883, a merger involving the Edison company created General Electric. Morgan underwrote the company's initial stock offering and got a seat on the GE board.

Edison got rich in this merger, took his profits, and invested them in his true love — invention. GE profits funded his work on batteries, motion picture projectors, and a host of other devices. He never seemed much interested in fortune. It was not where his heart lay. When asked many years later where all the money went he said, "Well, it's all gone, but we had a hell of a good time spending it." Exciting things happen in mega-markets.

STEEL AND OIL

Two other major industries grew in the first mega-market. Both provided enormous competition to existing, Old Economy businesses. Steel overwhelmed the iron and metals industries. And oil refineries provided an energy source that was soon recognized as cleaner, more efficient, and more flexible in its uses than the staple, coal.

Commercial steel was made in the United States as early as 1856, but large-scale production was not begun until the final year of the Civil War. As with all new things, it took hold gradually. But by the early 1870s it became clear that harder, stronger steel rails would make it possible for railroads to carry much heavier loads, making each train more efficient. No one grasped the financial value of this change more readily than Andrew Carnegie, who had already invested in railroad equipment companies that made iron axles for freight cars and rails for new lines.

Carnegie stands out as the prototypical American success story. He emigrated from Scotland to the United States with his family in 1848. A poor family, the Carnegies settled in Allegheny, outside Pittsburgh, and young Andrew was sent to work in a textile mill at age fourteen. By age sixteen he was writing letters to relatives in Scotland, telling them about the railroads coming to Pittsburgh and the excitement he felt. Burning with ambition, he became a telegraph clerk, and then secretary to the superintendent of the Pennsylvania Railroad. He borrowed against his mother's house to invest in hot stocks. Profit from that venture went into the purchase of one of the region's first gushing oil wells. By age thirty, he was rich.

At the end of the Civil War, Carnegie had the wisdom to see the age of iron was passing and the fortune to invest in its usurper, steel. Convinced that the country was on the verge of an almost endless period of growth, and that steel would be needed to build railroads, bridges, skyscrapers, and more, Carnegie set about building an enormous foundry in Braddock, a suburb of Pittsburgh. The mill was placed on the banks of the Monongahela River, where supplies of iron ore, coke, and coal were readily off-loaded from barges, and finished steel could be shipped out. The Braddock works would eventually have eighteen huge furnaces that worked twenty-four hours a day.

It's hard to imagine that Carnegie truly expected what would happen when he began construction of that first mill. In fact, America's demand for steel would grow fiftyfold during the first mega-market. Through most of this period, the biggest supplier would be Carnegie. This was thanks to the Civil War veteran who would supply much of the genius, energy, and leadership needed to make Carnegie's steel mill run.

Captain William "Bill" Jones was a physically commanding man with a personality to match. As superintendent of the Braddock plant, Jones made key improvements in the steel making process and machinery. Despite a lack of formal education, Jones made several discoveries in the chemistry of steel making and was acclaimed, even in Europe, as a master engineer. As talented as he was, Jones was also charismatic. He was constantly on the mill floor, getting his hands dirty to fix problems. His example inspired a workforce of thousands to increase their output almost continually. The profits that flowed to Carnegie from this one plant eventually exceeded 130 percent of his investment per year. The only company that grew bigger, and faster, in the first mega-market, was John D. Rockefeller's Standard Oil.

John D. Rockefeller was a merchant in Cleveland when the first oil rush in history struck Western Pennsylvania. This wasn't a case of oil suddenly being discovered and exploited. Generations of locals knew about the oil that oozed out of the ground and floated on a creek in

Titusville. But it wasn't until chemists figured out how to refine the stuff into a burnable fuel — initially kerosene was used as a source of light — that it became valuable. And even then, someone had to figure out an efficient way to collect enough of the stuff for a commercially viable refinery. This someone was a middle-aged prospector named Edwin Drake. It was Drake, working for a New Haven banker, who decided to drill into the earth in Titusville and saw the oil bubble up.

While others flocked to the Pennsylvania hills, where a forest of derricks arose, John D. Rockefeller invested enough to acquire 50 percent ownership in an early refinery. He was perfectly located. Cleveland was nearer to the oil fields than any other major city and, with access to railroads, it was the perfect place to set up a facility for buying crude, refining it, and shipping the kerosene across the country. The plant was built on a small river that led, eventually, to Lake Erie. Able to ship by water or rail, Rockefeller held a distinct advantage. Unlike others, he would never be captive to arbitrary increases in freight charges. He always had an alternative.

The price of oil fluctuated wildly in the early days. New finds — wells that produced thousands of barrels of oil per day — produced gluts on the market. When refinery capacity eventually expanded enough to handle the flow, shortages developed. The chaos decimated many companies, and Rockefeller began buying them up. To avoid charges of monopoly — which was, in fact, what he was creating — Rockefeller collected these businesses in what was called a trust.

Many of Rockefeller's methods and collusions — especially with railroads — are illegal today. He used excessive pressure to get retailers to buy his products and he undercut competitors with a ruthlessness not seen before, or since. If this sounds familiar, it may be because one of today's major technologies — personal computers

— is dominated by a single company that neither makes the machine nor sells it. Gaining the middle ground between a new technology and its consumers is always profitable.

Fascinating as Rockefeller was, what is important about his business, from our point of view, is how it grew under the conditions of the mega-market. The oil business endured many short-term retrenchments as price cuts and competition stalled the growth of individual companies. But Rockefeller rode out these downturns, and followed the overriding upward trend in the business. In a relatively short time, he exploited a technology that had not even existed when he was born, to become the world's richest man. His empire reached into almost every business sector.

CHAOS AND ORDER

The stories of the Captains of Industry make compelling biographies. Even in their time, they were each the subject of many books. But these men and their lives also help explain the evolution of the first mega-market. The capital that they created was invested in a myriad of industries. This can be seen in the steady rise in the volume of shares traded on the New York Stock Exchange. In 1875, annual trading was roughly 54 million shares. Ten years later, average annual volume exceeded 85 million. The profits that could be made in trading stocks in New York attracted investments from the major national banks around the world. In a scenario that would be repeated during future mega-markets, the value of the stocks of new boom industries grew much faster than the profits of the companies themselves. The real value was seen in the future, and investors competed with each other to hold a piece of it.

Of course, all of the activity created opportunity for speculators and swindlers, too. One of the more notorious cases involved Ulysses S. Grant and his family. They were drawn into creating an investment house, which at first profited on the Grant name. His partner soon developed a Ponzi scheme, borrowing money to buy stocks and borrowing more to pay off the debts. A dip in the market made it impossible for him to pay margin calls. The firm went bust, and Grant lost much of his family fortune.

Despite the occasional disaster, like Grant's, the market functioned effectively, providing capital for the development of new businesses and returns for investors. Large European companies kept out of the American market by tariffs on products such as steel, nevertheless found a way to make money in the States by investing in stocks. In 1885, the value of common stocks exceeded the value of bonds for the first time in U.S. history.

The stunning growth of the American economy was also helped by monetary policy. Protectionist laws shielded U.S. industry from foreign competition. Government policies were key to bringing order to chaos in New Economy businesses. Through land grants and subsidies, railroads grew across the land. Utilities were permitted to develop into monopolies. And before antitrust legislation, the absence of controls allowed Standard Oil to become a remarkably efficient enterprise, controlling its product all the way from the field through to its sale to consumers.

One final, and critical, element provided fuel for the first megamarket: immigration. From 1870 to 1890, the U.S. population grew from 38.5 million to 63 million. Ten million of these new Americans were immigrants. They were mainly Germans, Italians, Eastern Europeans, and Jews from all of Europe. The newcomers, including my grandparents, settled mainly in big cities where they found work in new industries. New York, for example, saw a doubling of its factories during the first mega-market. Their capitalization grew from roughly $150 million in 1870 to more than $450 million in 1890. The factory workforce rose 49 percent.

These factories were needed to produce an array of industrial and consumer products that grew bigger every day. Inventions literally flooded the country. One measure of this was the number of patents granted by the U.S. Patent Office. In the seventy years preceding the Civil War, a grand total of 36,000 patents were issued. During the first mega-market, nearly that many were granted every single year.

Many of these patents were issued for products that simply entertained or enlightened. The first mega-market coincided with and helped to create the social period called the Gilded Age, and there was plenty of money available for sport and luxury. After all, 4,000 millionaires had been created by the business boom, and they were eager to spend.

Tycoons competed to see who had the biggest and most lavishly appointed city homes, country estates, and yachts. The New York Yacht Club's register of vessels grew from twenty-nine boats in 1882 to seventy-one by 1890. Each new boat seemed to be larger and more opulent. Morgan's second Corsair, a steel-hulled beauty that was 241 feet in length, had eight staterooms complete with baths and fireplaces. But the most impressive yacht of the time was probably the *Aphrodite*, a 303-footer owned by the treasurer of Standard Oil, Oliver H. Payne.

Mark Twain, who was the most recognized writer of the era, satirized this society and coined its nickname in his very first novel, *The Gilded Age*, which was published in 1873. It was filled with satires of the rich and the ambitious. It contains scenes from the Wild West and tales of political corruption that mirrored real scandals of the day. The most memorable character in the book was a con man named Col. Beriah Sellers who always believed that a $1 million fortune waited around the corner.

The Gilded Age was a hugely successful book and became a popular stage play. But its biting commentary did not dim the excitement of the times. While the rich indulged in every luxury imaginable — and even invented a few — there were also plenty of amusements for the not-so-rich. (Spare cash was available for this fun because, as of 1870, the average American wage exceeded the cost of living.) Photography studios spread to the smallest towns. A bicycle craze filled the streets with high-wheelers. Gymnastics and basketball were popular among men and women. Fraternal organizations such as the Moose and Odd Fellows grew. Park systems, as well as schools and free libraries, were opened to serve the public. The titans of industry were an enormous part of this effort, donating millions of dollars to the cause. Most of this largess came from a genuine concern for society.

Behind the fortunes of these men lay the real source of the great expansion of the economy, the increase in the standard of living, and America's rise among nations: the mega-market. But like all bull markets, it eventually ran out of energy.

A CHANGE IN MOOD

The beginning of the end of the first mega-market was foreshadowed by a change in the public mood. By the end of the 1880s, the message Twain delivered about the dangers of greed and corruption was starting to take hold. A series of scandals — some involving industrialist Jay Gould — cost thousands of investors their fortunes and many more their jobs.

Inflation had begun to increase in the late 1880s as tariffs kept out foreign competition and allowed domestic manufacturers to raise prices almost at will. In the West, farmers were outraged by increases demanded for such basics as shoes, sugar, and tools. Local politicians played on their resentments with a new, anti–big business populism.

In 1890, in response to public outcry about the Standard Oil trust and others, the first antitrust act was passed to begin to regulate these monopolies. In that same year a second key law, the Sherman Silver Act, tied the dollar, in part, to silver instead of gold. The market's response was predictable. Worried that the U.S. currency's link to gold was being broken, foreign investors began dumping their stocks.

A keen observer would have detected the inflation and other shifts that were going to end the mega-market. First, Washington was exerting power over the market, and this had to be considered a bad omen. Second, the pace of technological and infrastructure growth was slowing. Railroads had reached all the important cities, as well as the key areas where agriculture and natural resources like oil and timber needed to be shipped. Every state and territory was served. Third, foreign investors had begun to sell. If you recall the four phases of price activity, this trend indicated a coming decline in prices. Negative momentum was building.

The psychology of the market was further weakened when it was revealed that the federal government's gold reserves were dwindling. This caused U.S. investors to panic. In February 1893 the New York Stock Exchange saw its busiest day of trading ever — 1.5 million shares — and the index fell to an all-time low. In coming months, more than 500 banks would collapse, and 15,000 businesses would go bankrupt, including almost one third of all railroads. In many places in rural America you can find remnants of these companies, actually pieces of track that are long abandoned and lead to nowhere

In the first mega-market the wisest investors were not ruined by the Panic of 1893 because they had already recognized that the mega-market was over. They profited by sector gains of 400 percent or more! But even an investor in the overall market would have made 200 percent in the years between 1877 and 1891.

The story of the first mega-market, and the factors that created it, establish a model that we will see replicated three more times. I call this the footprint of a mega-bull market. It is illustrated with a graph that compares two industries of the day. I think it explains why many on Wall Street failed to take full advantage. In the graph below, the Old Economy mining and smelting stocks languish while the New Economy railroad equipment stocks flourish.

RAILROAD EQUIPMENT VERSUS MINING & SMELTING 1876–1891

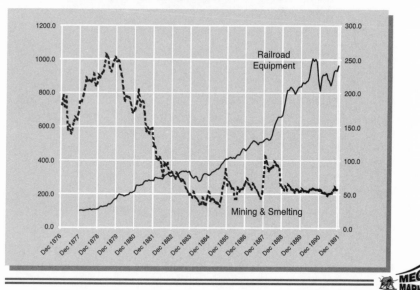

Today the same dynamic is at work, the bull market is not treating all sectors equally. Old Economy stocks — traditional retailers, manufacturers, and basic materials companies who refuse to adapt — are treading water while the technology infrastructure stocks flourish. In essence, a bull and a bear market coexist. You will see the footprint again.

CHAPTER 5

THE SECOND MEGA-MARKET: 1921–1929

JUST MENTION THE 1920s and most people leap to the same association — the stock market crash of 1929. The impulse is certainly
understandable, and almost uncontrollable. And the images that arise
are more than a little disturbing: investors ruined, brokerage houses
closed, and the start of an economic period so terrible that it's called,
simply, The Great Depression.

For many of us the instant connection between the '20s and the
Crash is based on something more than dry history. It is personal.
Members of my family lived through the hard times that followed in
the 1930s. Even if they did not lose their homes or businesses, they
felt the fear and the pinch. Pasta and beans replaced meat on my family's dinner table and on most tables in our neighborhood.

But even though the Crash brought in a period of hardship, my
family did not forget the great fun that people had in the decade leading up to October 1929. My father was a young man back then, and he
had a very good time in New York during the period of speakeasies

and flappers. He went to the Cotton Club in its glory days, and held on to wonderful memories of the great music of the time and the glamour that was all around.

Today, as a technical analyst who has studied history to understand the modern market, I look back and see that the Roaring Twenties tell me much more about today than the Crash. All the glitter was a reflection of a truly remarkable period of growth that constituted the second mega-market. Between 1921 and 1929, the Dow Jones Industrial average climbed 465 percent. This took place on the strength of a technology-driven New Economy based primarily on automobiles and electric devices, especially radio.

Yes. I know how it ended. And right now I can hear you asking — Will today's bull market end the same way?

I don't think so.

I base this conclusion on two major factors. First, the Crash of 1929 occurred in a financial environment that was radically different from today's. The kind of speculation and outright manipulation of stocks permitted then is impossible now. Second, the information available today, to every regulator and investor, means we have a far more rational financial marketplace.

The actual causes of the Crash are still debated. But it is clear that inflation was an important factor and so, too, were rapidly rising interest rates caused by the great demand for funds to cover an excessive volume of margin trades on the stock exchange. Foreign investors who pulled their money out of American banks played a role, as did the Federal Reserve Bank. In the end, a series of events that could not be repeated today occurred, ending the second mega-market.

Too often overlooked is the fact that even with the panic of the stock market plunge, there were many investors who read the signs, saw the mega-market coming to a close, and protected much of what they had gained during the run-up. Joseph P. Kennedy saved his fortune by selling in 1928, when he thought the market had gone about as high as it could go. Bernard Baruch made similar moves in early 1929.

Later in the book, I will further address the skeptics who believe that the current mega-market is going to end with a Crash. I think the current mega-market could eventually end with a whimper. It should be similar to the end of the third mega-market, when we saw a gradual unwinding of stock prices, with shares basically trending lower, or moving sideways for years.

But even if I am wrong about this — and I don't think I am — remember that this is one of the reasons you study technical factors in the first place. They can give you an indication when the market is about to change.

THE FIRST WORLD WAR

During the second mega-market, Baruch, Kennedy, and thousands of investors profited from all of the factors I consider hallmarks of a mega-market. The first, and most important, was the peace that followed the end of World War I. Peace is always bullish.

America was drawn reluctantly into the First World War. The conflict started in 1914, but nearly three years would pass before the first Americans saw fire. Modern technologies — machine guns, poison gas, and quick-firing artillery — made the battlefields even more horrific than those of the Civil War. The machine gun, far superior to Gatling's original invention, was fearsome. At the start of the war German troops were much better trained in its use. In an early battle on the Western front, the Allies lost 8,000 men in less than four hours, mainly to the German machine gun crews. German losses were exactly zero. Airplanes and tanks were introduced to war, but they were not very effective. The trucks and ships built to transport troops were far more vital. Much of what we consider modern manufacturing — high volume assembly lines, outsourcing — was developed to meet the demands of the war. Shipyards underwent a virtual revolution in manufacturing methods as, for the first time, sections of ships were built off-site and then transported to yards to be fitted together.

At home, more than 4 million men donned uniforms. This was seven times the number that the Army was prepared to clothe, house, and feed. As a result, huge camps were built, increasing demand for wood, nails, and cement, and employing 200,000 craftsmen. (The barracks they built were, for many recruits, more luxurious than their own homes. Plenty of young boys first got regular access to a flush toilet when they joined up.) Baruch was made chairman of the War Industries Board, which oversaw 35,000 companies that made everything from socks (130 million pairs) to rifles (2.5 million).

While thousands of small factories worked overtime to fill orders for basic goods and arms, many heavy manufacturing companies were built out of the war effort. Hundreds of ships were launched, all of them requiring tons of steel and sophisticated equipment. Wireless radio, which Guglielmo Marconi had invented only fifteen years earlier, was required for every vessel. Bakelite, the first plastic, was manufactured in greater amounts, and a new process for refining oil — thermal cracking — dramatically improved the production of fuels.

Far more important than the production, machines, and inventions was the human experience of the war. Since the battle was never waged on our continent, America was spared the direct damage to infrastructure and civilian morale. And just over 122,000 Americans died in the war, a horrific toll but not even one third the number in the War Between the States. In 1919, 3 million able-bodied men came home from the conflict. They had all matured in the service, acquired skills, and been exposed to a much bigger world than they had imagined before. Hence the song lyric "How do you keep them down on the farm after they've seen gay Paree?"

The country they discovered on their return had changed, too. So many workers had flocked to the cities to take jobs in war-related industries that, for the first time, more people lived in urban areas than in the country. American industry grew to account for more than half of all manufacturing worldwide. Profits increased, and so did investment in plants and equipment. The wealth trickled down, too. Wages had more than doubled since 1914, greatly expanding the middle class.

Prohibition had outlawed alcohol and instantly created a black market in drink. In the soldiers' absence, a women's movement had gained considerable ground. In 1920 women got the vote, through the Nineteenth Amendment, and many had been employed in the war effort. But the most colorful changes were in the way women dressed, and acted. The hemlines on skirts were raised and the necklines on blouses were lowered. Women now smoked in public and drank gin in the privacy of the speakeasies.

The restless energy of the doughboys was soon to find outlets in the twin engines of the second mega-market. The first was the automobile. It would carry a generation into a prosperity never seen before. The second was the radio. It would provide the rhythm of the age.

THE AUTOMOBILE AGE

As always happens with mega-markets, the peace and prosperity that followed war did not emerge immediately. When the government stopped buying war material, many industries saw orders dry up. What some analysts call an "inventory recession" began in January 1920 and ran into the middle of 1921.

From its bottom in 1921, the Dow Jones Industrial Average witnessed six strong years with an average gain of 27.9% and two down years with an average loss of –1.8%. By the time it peaked in 1929, the DJIA managed to gain a total of 496%. There were twenty-five noticeable rallies (gains of 10% or more) that averaged 18.3% and extended, on average, for a little over 3 1/2 months. There were twenty-five declines that averaged –8.9% and lasted slightly more than a month in length. The biggest rally scored an 83.4% gain. The worst sell off was a –18.7% decline. The Dow's best year was 1928, up 48.2%, while its worst year was 1923, down –3.2%. There were also extended periods when the Dow was frustratingly neutral.

THE DOW JONES INDUSTRIALS
1921–1929

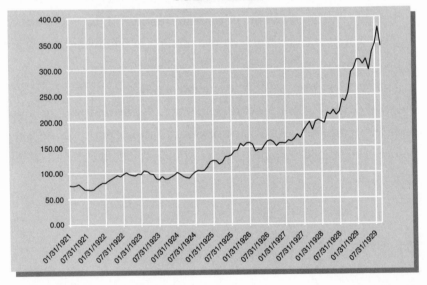

The second mega-market was stimulated, in part, by the homecoming soldiers who fortunately managed to find jobs and establish homes. Their discharge and bonus pay made them flush with cash. Meanwhile, many households redeemed the Liberty Bonds they had purchased to support the war. What did people buy with all this money? Cars.

In the industry's infancy, which lasted from 1890 to about 1910, literally hundreds of automobile companies were begun — many in bicycle shops and barns — by entrepreneurs who convinced eager investors that they were going to capitalize on the next new thing. With names like Franklin, Kisselcar, Brush, and Jack Rabbit, the majority of these companies went out of business entirely. A few were absorbed by the more successful manufacturers.

Innovation was constant. The Dusenbergs got their start by attaching a motor to a pair of bikes. British immigrant Alexander Winton put his on an old horse buggy. In 1897, people were so skeptical about the future of these vehicles that when Winton actually managed to drive one of his buggies from Cleveland to New York City, no one in New York would believe it.

Doubt and criticism dogged the early car business. Even the combustion engine was a source of controversy in the early years. Before the gas engine won out, more than 100 manufacturers made steam cars, and nearly as many produced electric vehicles. The cars were expensive — starting at around $20,000 in today's dollars for the cheapest — and they were in short supply. In 1903, Ford, Buick, and Cadillac made fewer than 5,000 all together.

But there were advances made. Tillers were replaced by steering wheels. The shortcomings of electric and steam were eventually accepted by everyone. As the gasoline engine came to dominate, the center of manufacturing settled in the Midwest. This was where the majority of gas engine makers had been founded years earlier to serve farm equipment companies. It made sense that the car makers would set up shop near them.

As the superior designs began to dominate, it also became clear that large-scale, assembly line–style manufacturing would push prices down, making more sales possible. But as always happens when a daring new technology emerges, many people wedded to the Old Economy fail to adapt. Of all people, J. P. Morgan, who recognized the value of energy, railroads, and steel in the 1880s, could not see how big the automobile would become.

In 1908, when the famous William "Billy" Durant was trying to pull a handful of companies together to form what would become General Motors, he went to Morgan for financing. Durant, who at five foot five and 130 pounds was called by some "little Billy," believed that GM would eventually sell 500,000 cars a year. With car prices about equal to the average worker's annual salary, Morgan couldn't accept Durant's estimate.

Morgan believed he had arithmetic on his side. In all of the country there were fewer than 150,000 cars. That was one per fifty families. Morgan himself preferred horse-drawn carriages to cars, which all rich men owned, but he regarded them as akin to yachts. They were flashy, enjoyable, but impractical and would never suit the masses. He sent Durant away.

(Morgan's rejection of the automobile is a classic example of an executive's failure to reinvent himself to benefit from a New Economy. He was sixty-eight years old at the time he made this decision, and apparently just could not appreciate how much people would love the power, the freedom, and the beauty of automobiles.)

Though Durant failed to win Morgan's money, he managed to put together the General Motors deal anyway, combining Oldsmobile, Buick, Cadillac, and Oakland Motor Car, which eventually became Pontiac. Soon other companies, including parts and body manufacturers, were added. Within two years, GM was making and selling 50,000 cars per year. The firm became the main competitor for Ford, which produced three times as many cars. Henry Ford kept slashing prices on his single car, the Model T. For its part, GM offered more variety and innovation, capturing that part of the market that was not driven strictly by price.

By the time the First World War began, J. P. Morgan's dismissive attitude about the automobile was proven wrong. More than 2.5 million cars were on the roads. The public demanded better quality and lower prices. This drove many companies out of business. Of the 300 manufacturers who sold vehicles in 1910, fewer than fifty remained in 1917. (They fell by the wayside like so many of today's dot-com start-ups.) Even fewer would be in the marketplace when the war ended, and the second mega-market began. But their importance cannot be discounted. J. P. Morgan notwithstanding, the automotive stocks experienced astounding growth.

During this period GM's sales grew to 500,000 cars per year. This increase was accomplished, in large part, with the introduction of credit buying. For years a few manufacturers had offered installment plans, but it wasn't until Durant created the General Motors Acceptance Corporation in 1920 that great numbers of people began to finance cars. By the end of the decade, more than 70 percent of all cars were bought this way.

Ironically, GMAC and other innovations took root just as Billy Durant was losing control of GM. He was ousted in the market dip of 1920–21. (This despite the fact that the company he built — GM — was doing very well.) Though temporarily set back, Durant remained at the center of the action. In the spring of 1921, before anyone knew that the economy was going to rev into overdrive, Little Billy announced he was starting a brand new company — Durant Motors — to be capitalized with $5 million in stock. The price per share was $10.

Billy Durant was a man who would have succeeded in any time, but his optimistic, frenetic personality was a perfect match for the mood of the '20s and the second mega-market. In the towns where he had previously built GM plants, and employed thousands of workers, people with money to invest believed in him, and people with the money to buy cars did too. His initial public offering was snapped up quickly, and before he even had a factory, he had orders for more than $30 million worth of cars.

Durant didn't disappoint. He quickly bought two plants from the Goodyear tire company, which had been hit hard by the market dip. Once he had these facilities, it took less than sixty days for him to design and build a prototype car. Even as he dashed around the country, arranging to buy engines here and axles there, Durant took time to sell his vision of the automotive future. He saw roads being built everywhere, wages rising, and the prices for cars falling. The industry was still in its infancy, he told reporters, and the growth in the years to come would far exceed what had happened to date.

Durant was more accurate than any psychic could possibly have been. By the end of the second mega-market, 60 percent of all households owned a car. Price would guarantee the automobile's success. Between 1913 and 1923, the Model T would drop from $600 to $398. Most other models would follow a similar trend. Even the luxury Packard would drop from $4,150 to $2,885.

On the last day of 1922 — with the mega-market just a few months old — Durant Motors loaded 500 cars from its Long Island City, New York, plant on a special freight train bound for California. It was called the Prosperity Special and it was a brilliant publicity stunt for Durant Motors.

The publicity would have meant nothing if the cars didn't sell. But price and quality combined to make sales easy. Quality was probably the more important of the two. In the beginning, cars had been unreliable and even dangerous to operate. A crank starter could break your arm if the engine happened to backfire. But by 1920, cars like

Durant's models had evolved into the basic machines we drive today. They were reliable and easy to operate.

Again, the computer is a good analogy. In the early 1970s, computers were large, hugely expensive, and difficult to operate. A personal computer wasn't even on the drawing boards. But creative technological improvements would steadily drive down prices and make computers far more accessible and reliable. Eventually, we would have a machine that anyone could use, and it would become the engine of a mega-market.

Little Billy's engine, the Durant Motors Co., was so powerful that investors fought to be part of the action. Within two years the stock price climbed to $84. Well aware of the need for high volume to keep his prices competitive with Ford, Durant gobbled up parts companies and other car makers. He grabbed the Connecticut-based Locomobile company out of bankruptcy so he could have a luxury model to sell. And he bought a truck manufacturer, to take advantage of the New Economy's demand for alternatives to rail. Trucks were more vital to the growth of the time than most people recognize. They made deliveries faster, and like the Internet today, greatly expanded the market area a business could serve. Suddenly a paint store in Minneapolis would compete with a paint store in St. Paul. The new competition may have squeezed inefficient operators out of business but it also drove prices down.

THE MARKET AS A WHOLE

It's hard to overstate what Billy Durant accomplished in the early years of the mega-market. He leveraged an idea — Durant Motors — and his gut instinct about the industry to create a business that employed almost 50,000 people in factories across the country. He sold 75,000 cars in less than two years. This reflected the huge run-up on total car sales, and the stocks associated with this business climbed right along. Naturally that included companies that made steel, glass, rubber, and even the equipment and materials to build roads.

A look at the sector by sector breakdown of the market during the years 1921 to 1929 (on the opposite page) shows how strong the whole economy was. The poorest performing group, the Old Economy oil stocks, gained just 153 percent. Automobiles, with all the competition and consolidation that went on, rose an amazing 1076.5 percent. But note below that from 1922 to 1924 there was very little movement in any direction.

STANDARD & POOR'S AUTOMOBILE GROUP

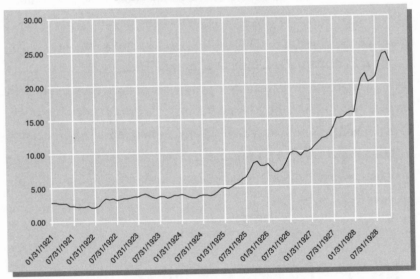

As you can see, a great many stocks soared in the second mega-market, and that made a certain segment of the population very rich. This is one reason why the mythology that grew up around the Roaring Twenties is dominated by the wretched excesses of New

York's elite as portrayed by F. Scott Fitzgerald. But this is not an accurate picture of how the mega-market affected the nation. Even at the end of the boom, only 28 percent of Americans owned any stock at all. The average American experienced the second mega-market less directly, watching his local business improve and enjoying a higher income. Real disposable income grew by 26 percent between 1922 and 1929. That's the magic of a mega-market; it affects the whole country positively, not just investors.

Because most of the Americans who benefited from the second mega-market were middle class, it was not the residents of Fitzgerald's West Egg but rather Sinclair Lewis's George Babbitt who mirrors the national experience. In Babbitt, America found a man delighted to be floating higher on a prosperity he didn't quite understand. A real-estate salesman, he boosted his hometown shamelessly, and if he was the subject of ridicule, he was also a true representative of his hustling age. And yes, he loved motorcars.

THE PERFORMANCE OF ALL TEN S&P GROUPS DURING THE 1921/1929 MEGA-MARKET:

Group	Gain
Automobiles	+ 1076.5%
Retail, Department Stores	+ 786.0
Utilities — Electric Companies	+ 700.9
Banks — Money Center	+ 646.5
Footware	+ 494.4
Iron & Steel	+ 343.2
Paper & Forest Products	+ 236.7
Tobacco	+ 246.7
Railroads	+ 155.2
Oil — Composite	+ 153.0

I love cars too. If you don't believe it, consider the story of a special bonus I received from my employer, Prudential, when the Dow Jones Industrial Average had just passed 7,000. When my boss asked me what I might like as a reward I said, half joking, "A 1962 Corvette, Roman red." A couple of weeks later, the car was mine. A rich kid at my college had this very car and I'd always lusted after it. For me this car represents the time in which it was built and our times too, the excitement and energy.

THE RHYTHM OF THE AGE

By itself, the automobile would have been enough to power the stock exchange of 1921–29 to mega-market status. But a second technology came along that also provided a tremendous boost to economic growth: radio.

Experimental radio stations operated as early as 1910, when Enrico Caruso's performance at the Metropolitan Opera House in New York was aired for a few dozen crude receiving sets. Of course, the quality of the weak signals transmitted in the early days was terrible. It was often impossible to pick up the sound over the static. (It was not unlike the first live Web broadcast of Wall Street research that I did for Prudential — it aired over the Internet. The transmission was a bit wobbly, but it foreshadowed a technology that one day will be perfected.)

Almost all radio traffic in the early days was confined to the dots and dashes of Morse code. The "radio telegraph" improved transatlantic communication and was vital to ocean liners, which were the only mode of travel across the sea. On April 12, 1912, this was made dramatically clear to the world when the *Titanic* struck an iceberg and began to sink. Radio telegraph messages sent by the distressed ship made it possible for nearby vessels to rescue hundreds of passengers.

The telegraph told the world the shocking news that the unsinkable *Titanic* was going down. The drama of this event is well known. But few people are old enough to recall that radio-telegraph offices were mobbed, and telegraph officers were the only source of information about events. Marconi, who happened to be in New York and actually held a ticket to return to Europe on the *Titanic*, made sure to play up his invention's role in saving lives. Newspapers picked up Marconi's point, and after the *Titanic* disaster, top-notch wireless communications systems became a must for all passenger liners.

The radio telegraph would get an even bigger push from the U.S. government during World War I. At the war's start, the United States made an extraordinary move into radio. It commandeered both the experimental stations and the huge commercial facilities that had been built along the East Coast — mostly in Massachusetts and New York — to send and receive wireless cables. The seizures were more important than many Americans realized. One German-owned station, in Sayville, Long Island, had been relaying encoded orders to the Kaiser's submarines in the North Atlantic. The German station and all the others were soon put to work on government and military messages among the United States, its Atlantic fleet, and Europe.

Though the seizure of radio stations was vital to the war effort, another element of the government's takeover was far more important to the economy. When the war broke out, the development of the radio industry was practically frozen by lawsuits over patents. Inventors and corporations that held patents on key components were suing each other. It was a legal miracle that anyone at all could build a little transmitter or a receiver for sound. (A similar situation exists today with battles over access to cable systems and broad band technologies.)

But with the outbreak of the war, the government simply set aside the patents that inventors had jealously protected and suspended the litigation. The Navy ordered thousands of radio telegraphs for its ships and land facilities. The Army needed both fixed stations and receivers and a new portable type "suitable to be carried by horse."

When the war ended, the U.S. Navy, which had done most of the work on radio, controlled dozens of new patents and employed most of the talented engineers. Key members of Congress were deeply worried that the American Marconi Company, founded by the Italian radio pioneer, would be subject to outside harmful foreign interests. Owen Young, then head of General Electric, offered a solution — a new company that would be called Radio Corporation of America. RCA would buy out Marconi and assume the Navy's patents. GE would be its single largest shareholder.

RCA began with tremendous technological and patent advantages, but its biggest asset turned out to be the managers and engineers of the Marconi Company. One, David Sarnoff, had been the old man's protégé. He was at the telegraph in New York when the *Titanic* sank, and handled hundreds of messages. And he had predicted, as far back as 1916, that radio would become "a household utility" around the world. At the time, very few people accepted this idea, and Sarnoff was dismissed. But he was the visionary who understood the New Economy was coming.

In RCA's early days, Sarnoff resurrected his idea of a "household utility" in a memo that his superiors had asked him to write laying out the future of the industry. He intended to show how RCA could become the biggest radio company in the world. The growth, as he saw it, would come in "radio music boxes" to be purchased by consumers. He predicted that if RCA could develop a reliable set, at a cost of about $75, 1 million could be sold in three years.

Sarnoff knew the radio business better than anyone. At the bottom rungs, he was a member of the association that linked hobbyists and amateur broadcasters. At the top of the business, he was on a first-name basis with every major scientist and engineer. He could see that radio had the power to captivate people and hold them transfixed. It was as powerful as the automobile. And he also recognized that the technology was evolving so rapidly that cheap, quality equipment would soon be available. But just as Sarnoff was trying to convince RCA's directors that music boxes were the future, Westinghouse — RCA's main competitor — began broadcasting from the two first commercial stations in the country, KDKA in Pittsburgh and WWJ in Detroit. Stations in New York, Chicago, and Boston quickly followed. In the race to broadcasting, RCA was left at the starting gate. (RCA was sort of like IBM in the 1970s when it didn't recognize the brilliance of Bill Gates and his operating system.)

Westinghouse executives had decided that once a signal was available, people would want to buy radios to hear it. They were right. In Pittsburgh stores began selling crude crystal receivers with little earpieces for as little as $10. In New York, similar sets were being made and sold for one third that price. Of course, the wealthy had options too. On the high end they could buy an Atwater Kent, which was really a beautiful piece of sculpture, made of wood, brass, and Bakelite, that happened to have a crude radio receiver in it.

In Massachusetts, Westinghouse itself set up a big plant and began churning out crystal receivers that it would sell by the thousands. Radio became a national craze. Within two years more than 550 stations were opened and half a million sets were bought.

Though many executives fear it, competition does have a certain Darwinian magic. Smart managers who engage the opponent and adapt to the challenge make their companies stronger. This is exactly what happened in the computer business in the 1980s, when upstarts challenged IBM, and it is exactly what happened in radio. The Westinghouse initiatives gave Sarnoff proof that his original forecast was correct. The RCA board finally backed his plan to develop both broadcast stations and a "radio music box."

Once set loose, Sarnoff made the most of his opportunity. A big New York promoter had set up a heavyweight title match between Jack Dempsey and Georges Carpentier, a French war hero with a great following in America. Sarnoff built a radio station from scratch to broadcast the fight. On a scalding hot July day, more than 300,000 people, the largest audience in the history of the world, listened in. Dempsey knocked out Carpentier in the fourth round, which was good for Sarnoff because minutes later the transmitter literally melted into a mass of Bakelite and vacuum tubes. Saved by the bell.

From that moment on, RCA grew at a phenomenal rate. Using cash and RCA stock, Sarnoff developed the NBC broadcasting network and he purchased much of the new technology that was being developed. The RCA radio music box was an instant hit. Sales of all radios doubled almost every year. By 1928, the price of a good quality RCA set with a speaker that could be heard by a roomful of people, was below $70. The company sold 650,000 in a year. The following year it sold 842,000. And what of the company's stock? It started at $7 in 1924, soared to $85 in the summer of 1928, and reached $572 in 1929. At that time a popular ditty summed up the situation: "Whatever the price you have to pay, it's never too high for RCA."

Radio offered an astounding business and investment opportunity. But as I've said, the exciting elements of business and history are found in people's lives. Radio transformed life in America more radically than any previous technology because it changed the way people thought about their country. For the first time, a single voice could be heard in every corner of the country at the same time.

This was a breathtaking development. The words of great leaders and thinkers would no longer be filtered through newspaper reporters and editors. They would be broadcast directly to the entire nation. (Remind you of the Internet?) Of course, generally what poured out of the radio was hardly momentous. Sporting events, pop music, comedy sketches like those of Amos and Andy, and serial stories dominated the early networks.

Local radio programs ranged from the high — the New York Philharmonic — to the low — salesmen offering snake oils to small-town audiences. Just as today's businesses, no matter what their business, rush to build websites, many firms that had no obvious link to the radio business opened their own stations anyway. Banks, retail stores, hardware companies, dairies, and even farms had radio stations.

By the end of the mega-market, 13 million households had radio, and this new technology knit the country together with songs and words that were heard and repeated from coast to coast. Because networks were based in big cities, and jazz had become the music of the moment in urban centers, it also filled the airways around the country. Advertising was there, almost from the beginning, making it possible for the better broadcasting stations to become profitable.

Radio advertising helped create both modern ad campaigns and the national chain retailers. With access to a national market, manufacturers of everything from soda pop to cars began to use jingles and strategic placements of ads to broaden their name recognition. At the same time, retailers used the new medium to introduce themselves to new cities and towns. During the mega-market, the A&P grocery grew from 4,500 to 15,000 stores. Woolworth almost doubled in size, going from 1,000 to 1,825.

The new medium could build up personalities in the same way that it built businesses. Radio hosts and singers such as Rudy Valee attracted huge audiences when they appeared in public. But no one was bigger than Charles Lindbergh. His transatlantic flight foreshadowed one of the technologies that would drive future markets, the airplane. But at the moment it happened, it was seen as one man's heroic feat. Radio reports turned the man into a demigod. President Coolidge was besieged by proposals for honors. People wanted to name a star for Lindbergh. They wanted to put him on a stamp, grant him a lifetime exemption from taxes, and install him in the cabinet in a new position — secretary of aviation. (He got the stamp, becoming the first living person to be honored in this way.) Lindbergh became wealthy through his notoriety, and aviation stocks got a boost, too. Shares in the Wright Aeronautical Company rose from $25 to $245 in the eighteen months following the transatlantic crossing.

Overall, the radio contributed to a certain feeling in a country that had enjoyed more than a decade of peace and was reaping the benefits of wonderful new technologies. It was the background music, the beat behind a nation on the move. Looking back, it's easy to understand why many people — many investors — felt as if it could go on forever. If you look at the overall market at the time, this attitude is understandable. Stocks rose 200 percent from 1925 to 1928.

Of course, not everyone enjoyed the Roaring Twenties. As is always the case, the mega-market did not carry along every business. Agriculture suffered a particular hard go, as bankruptcies increased from under 2 percent of farms per year in 1920 to 18 percent in 1928. Farmers were caught in a strange new bind. Machinery and improved methods had made them more efficient. But as they produced more, prices went down. Unfortunately, since people can only eat so much, demand did not increase significantly. This was a conundrum that farming would wrestle with for the rest of the century.

THE OLD AND THE NEW

Two other enormous businesses — coal and the railroads — faltered in the second mega-market because they were stuck in the Old Economy and did not reinvent themselves. Coal lost a significant part of its business to oil and electricity. The railroads were pressured by the new over-the-road trucking industry, which could reach every doorstep in America with a direct shipment.

The technology represented by trucks meant that the Old Economy railroad stocks were eventually replaced by the new technology stocks of the day. For a clear view of how this phenomenon played out on Wall Street, look at my chart of the DJIA and the daily NYSE Advance/Decline Line (breadth).

Note the negative divergence between breadth and the Dow. Starting in 1925 these two lines began moving in opposite directions. Yes, even back in the 1920s there was a split between the "New and Old Economy" and it lasted for years.

The Advance/Decline Line helps us identify the direction of the majority of stocks. When the majority of stocks fail to confirm the strength of the leading blue chip stocks, the Dow Jones Industrial Average, the market's leadership is *said* to be too narrow and so the market's up trend is said to be not sustainable.

DOW JONES INDUSTRIALS WITH THE DAILY NYSE CUMULATIVE ADVANCE/DECLINE LINE
1925–1929

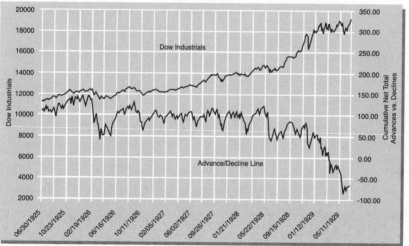

Ordinarily, three to six months of negative breadth — that is three to six months where there are more losers than winners when you plot the Advance/Decline Line — results in some kind of market sell-off or correction.

As discussed in Chapter 3, the accepted wisdom is that the stock market cannot keep going higher when there is a long stretch (measured in years) of negative breadth. But, again, I don't think this conventional wisdom applies to the mega-markets. In fact, negative breadth accompanied by a continued rise in the DJIA is typical of mega-markets. In the 1920s, an investor who recognized the footprint of the mega-market would have focused on the New Economy stocks or growth stocks and reaped tremendous benefits.

SIGNS OF TROUBLE

All engines eventually need tune-ups. This is what occurs when mega-markets experience dips that winnow out the weaker companies and deflate speculation. And eventually even the best markets run out of steam. This is what happened in 1929, after a long period of sustained overall growth. There were signs of what was to come, but most investors didn't pay attention. Like the rest of America, they were happily tooling along, with the radio playing. The crash hit them head-on, creating unprecedented financial and psychological trauma.

Looking back, it's possible to say that wise investors should have seen the signs of trouble. Beginning as early as 1927, margin-buying, in which investors borrowed from brokerages to get stock, began to climb quickly. In less than three years, margin loans rose from $3.5 billion to $8.5 billion, which was three times the federal budget. (By the way, margin-buying today is a concern but in relative terms is nowhere near as significant as it was in the 1920s. That's one of the reasons why I don't think a 1929-type crash will ever be repeated.) All of these loans were subject to immediate "call," which meant the brokers could demand repayment, with interest, the moment the stocks purchased on margin faltered. This is exactly what happened in October 1929.

About a month before the crash, William Hamilton, Charlie Dow's replacement as editor of *The Wall Street Journal*, applied Dow Theory to the market and concluded that the boom would soon be over. One telling development was that stocks were churning at ever greater volumes, suggesting speculation. In that time, so-called "pools" of investors were often formed around individual stocks. Each member would bid up the price of a holding, and then they would all sell at a profit. Illegal today, pools resemble the Internet-based chat groups that can, in a less formal way, drive today's high-tech stocks upward.

In 1928, a pool began churning up to 500,000 shares of RCA stock every day. (This was remarkable because, at the time, only 400,000 shares were available to trade.) In a week RCA rose 60 points. The pool got out with a $5 million profit. More notorious cases followed. When the small Kolster Radio Co. saw its stock fall, it hired a publicity expert to talk up the company and use cash, where necessary, to induce financial reporters to write favorable stories. A flurry of trading moved the stock from $74 to $95. Company directors took their profits. Kolster went bankrupt in little more than a year.

The incredible run-ups in some stocks led to a craze among small investors. Popular magazines published poems about stock tips and psychics sold newsletters predicting hot investments. Salesmen at investment houses used car registration lists to cold call for new customers. About 28 percent of Americans owned stocks in 1929, approximately double the percentage in 1900. (Today the figure is 40 percent.) When the market began to sour, many of these salesmen pleaded for their customers to hold on to their stocks, even as the stocks' worth disintegrated.

The Securities and Exchange Act would not be passed until 1933, as a post-Crash reform, so there was little the government could do to control unscrupulous salesmen and brokerages. For the full run of the second mega-market, Washington had kept its hands off of the market, adhering to Calvin Coolidge's declaration that "the business of America is business."

Herbert Hoover, newly installed in the White House, could hardly stop the crash once it started. For a time, key bankers slowed the crisis with large purchases of stocks at premium prices. But this only delayed the inevitable. The second mega-market ended in a uniquely disastrous way. The bad news was everywhere, and as far as most people could see, it was a disaster. Many auto companies, including Durant's, were undone by the crash, but the big three — Chrysler, GM, and Ford — would survive and thrive again.

Time heals all wounds, in markets as well as in people. RCA, which fell hard in 1929, remained healthy enough to begin constructing what was then the largest office building in the country at Rockefeller Center. (RCA's commitment may well have saved the Rockefeller project, and the Rockefeller family's fortune.) Television would provide the next big boom for the company, but before then, the U.S. economy would have to be pulled out of the Great Depression by a combination of Franklin Delano Roosevelt's New Deal and, the biggest factor of all, World War II.

Let's review what occurred in the second mega-market. We can see that once again, peace was bullish. Technologies and production methods developed and refined for the war effort were transferred to the peacetime marketplace. Peace made people optimistic, willing to buy new goods and willing to invest in the future represented by the stock market. It is interesting to notice that the drivers of the New Economy in the second mega-market were similar to those in the first.

This time the key transportation development was not trains, but cars and trucks. And the energy source was not oil, but electricity.

As in the first mega-market, government policies encouraged rapid business growth. Court rulings were generally favorable, and the federal taxes of wealthy investors were cut three different times — 1921, 1924, and 1926 — to stimulate investment. On the spending side, conservative policies meant a balanced federal budget, which dropped from $6.4 billion 1920 to a low of $3 billion in 1927. The national debt fell almost as sharply in the same period, from $25.5 billion at the start of the decade to $16.9 billion at the end. Clearly huge sums were freed for spending and lending in the private sector.

Improvements in what's called "human capital" were also at work in the second mega-market. Cities continued to grow as manufacturing jobs drew people out of small towns and farming regions. The education level of the average worker rose. Often overlooked are the improvements that were made in business management at this time. The companies that grew in the second mega-market were bigger and more complex than any before seen. In 1920 the Supreme Court ruled that size alone did not make these companies monopolies. But size did require more professional management, which often came from the upper ranks of the military. (RCA was dominated, in fact, by former Navy officers.)

The end of the second mega-market is not something that anyone would want to repeat, and structural changes make that unlikely. But its remarkable run confirms that the phenomenon of extended bull markets based on New Economy stocks is real. The economic story of the 1920s offers insight into today's mega-market and points to future growth in certain sectors. This is the valuable lesson of the second mega-market.

CHAPTER 6

THE THIRD MEGA-MARKET:
1949 – 1966

THE SECOND WORLD WAR occupies the largest section on the history shelves at my local library. Everyone knows the general outline of events — the military campaigns, Hitler's evil, the triumph of the Allies. It was both one of the most terrifying wars of all time and the most inspiring, for the courage and sacrifice it inspired. I don't need to recall history to evoke this period in our minds. We all know it, and we also feel it in our hearts.

The economic impact of World War II is less well known. Most of us understand that a tremendous industrial output was needed to beat the Axis, but for many of us our real knowledge begins and ends with Rosie the Riveter. Let's fill in some of the gaps with a few facts.

In 1937, when Franklin Delano Roosevelt began his second term, the country was probably more inward-looking, and more pacifist, than at any time in history. The problems of the Great Depression had required all of our energies, and we were beginning to recover. The public sector had played a major role, as Washington poured billions of dollars into roads, bridges and tunnels, rural electrification, and the construction of hydroelectric dams. Irrigation projects turned millions of desert acres into productive farmland.

Though government spending is never as good as the private sector when it comes to building the economy, these programs did create millions of jobs and built important infrastructure. With electric power and huge new tracts of fertile land opening in the West, agriculture became much more efficient. And the public services that were implemented — especially in transportation and electric power — would pay dividends for generations to come.

The late 1930s also saw the stock market recover much of its pre-Crash value. Though most big businessmen opposed Roosevelt-era regulations, these reforms probably ensured the long-term stability of the financial system. The Securities and Exchange Commission, first headed by Wall Street insider Joe Kennedy, became the watchdog that reassured investors that the stock exchanges were fair and honest. Full disclosure was required for stock offerings. Pools were outlawed. And federal deposit insurance, which was opposed by the American Bankers Association, was created to guarantee depositors that their money was safe. It permanently restored the public's faith in banks.

Across the Atlantic, another country that had been driven to its knees by the Depression responded quite differently. The Germans delayed in reforming their economy. Inflation was rampant. Employment was worse. Though it was by no means the only cause, economic chaos did contribute to the environment of fear that made Hitler possible. In 1937 Hitler repudiated the Treaty of Versailles and in 1938 he annexed Austria and Czechoslovakia. In April 1940 he rolled into Denmark and Norway and a full-scale continental war was underway. While Americans debated getting involved, he entered France. On June 14, 1940, the day Hitler took Paris, Roosevelt signed an order to more than double the U.S. Naval fleet. He had no doubt that we would be going to war.

For a year America served primarily as the "arsenal of democracy" providing billions of dollars worth of arms, food, and services. All this new production required huge investments in new plant and equipment. The government would eventually spend $9 billion to create plant capacity in private companies. (These modern facilities would of course, revert to private use at war's end.) Between 1939 and 1941 — prewar years — the gross national product would grow by an amazing 20 percent.

As we have seen in the wars leading to previous mega-markets, the industrial expansion that combat demands is also accompanied by innovation. In the late 1930s modern shipbuilding techniques were developed to reduce the time needed to build a Navy destroyer from one year to five months. (The famous Liberty ships, cargo vessels, could be turned out in a matter of days.) Nylon debuted in 1939 and would eventually become one of the most versatile substances on earth, used in everything from carpets to medical devices. (More than 60 million pair of women's nylon hose were sold in 1940, the first year they were made.) Improvements in aircraft meant that in 1939, Pan Am could inaugurate scheduled passenger service to Europe.

All this happened *before* America became a combatant. Once we actually joined the fighting, American output grew even faster. In March 1941, Britain and the United States began the massive Lend/Lease program. Six million workers were given jobs, wiping out unemployment. (Each fighting division in the field required 6,000 workers to supply it.) United States oil and synthetic rubber production soared. And under the burden of $350 billion in spending, the federal debt rose to $250 billion.

Allied scientists and inventors really got to work, too. Radar, pioneered by the British to detect incoming German planes and buzz bombs, was steadily refined to become accurate on land and sea and in the air. A cheap picture tube was developed, which would spur commercial TV after the war. RCA invented the electron microscope. The first jet planes were made. And penicillin was developed for human use. It eventually saved the lives of tens of thousands of soldiers.

(The development of penicillin, by British researchers, deserves a little extra attention here because it marked the true beginning of modern medicine. Up until this point, doctors had very few drugs at their disposal, and revolutionary medical breakthroughs occurred about once every century. Beginning with penicillin, this whole process would rev faster and faster, creating enormous health benefits, a huge new industry, and wonderful opportunities for investors.)

Of course, all of the other science and research done during World War II put together did not equal what was invested in and accomplished by the Manhattan Project. Conducted entirely in secret, this huge experiment led to the discovery of many new subatomic elements. It yielded the first large-scale nuclear reactor, the first plants for refining uranium and plutonium, and the first real computer, which was used for Manhattan Project calculations. Before they were done, the Manhattan Project engineers had built a series of industrial facilities that were larger than the entire U.S. auto industry. They had invented nuclear power plants, and, obviously, ended the war with the terrifying new weapon they had created.

THE POWER OF PEACE

As always happens, the end of the war brought tremendous relief to the national psyche. More than 5.5 million men came home to join the millions of others who had already been discharged. Once again, the nation worried about how soldiers would be integrated into civilian life, since the halt of wartime production meant that jobs were being eliminated. Federal spending, which had doubled the GNP during the war years, immediately dropped by 75 percent. An end to wartime wage and price controls led to a spike in prices. (Steak jumped from 50 cents a pound in 1945 to $1 in 1946.) Inflation drove the overall cost of living up 15 percent. And inflation was followed by a recession; economic growth slowed and unemployment rose. It would dampen the economy through 1948.

The country welcomed back its vets with the GI bill, which was going to have a much bigger impact than anyone could have expected. One of the main things it did was provide full college scholarships and living allowances for returning servicemen. Classrooms were soon filled with men preparing for jobs in a new, technology-driven society. They would become the best educated generation in history, precisely the kind of workers that the new, more sophisticated industries would need to keep growing.

While the veterans were off getting their college degrees, business and industry reorganized for a peacetime economy. A new global dynamic was emerging. America was the only major power that came out of the war with its landscape unscathed. Our industrial capacity was enormous. Our stock market was a magnet for international funds, and its major corporations would lead the reconstruction of Europe under the Marshall Plan. Under this plan, European nations were granted huge trade credits in order to import American goods. More than $80 billion would be spent on reconstruction projects, many of them carried out by American firms.

At home, pent-up urges for all sorts of things were being released. Millions of vets got married and immediately began families. This begat the baby boom, which would run for eighteen years and see 76 million children born. All of these babies would need to be fed, diapered, housed, transported, and educated. An unprecedented building boom began in the suburbs of every major city. All the demand — for housing, roads, schools, commercial services, and consumer goods — created millions of jobs.

By 1949, an American public that had known mainly sacrifice and deprivation for nearly twenty years was ready to enjoy postwar prosperity. In the coming decade, automobile sales would climb steadily, so that by the end of the '50s, 68 million cars were on the road, and 12 million families owned more than one. Automotive design catered to the craving for showy and yet powerful cars, and reflected the times. Huge tailfins and enormous engines dominated. The top of the line Cadillac even came with a perfume bottle and four gold-finished cups.

On Wall Street, the release of pent-up demand did wonders for certain stocks. Automobiles gained 932.2% between 1949 and 1966. The Household Furnishings and Appliances sector went up 717.1%

STANDARD & POOR'S
AUTOMOBILE GROUP 1947–1966

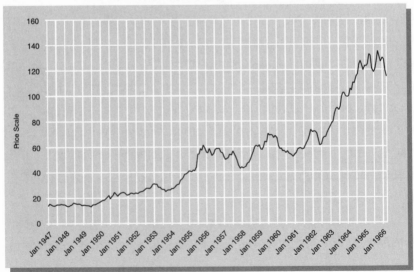

STANDARD & POOR'S
HOUSEHOLD FURNISHING APPLIANCES GROUP
1949–1966

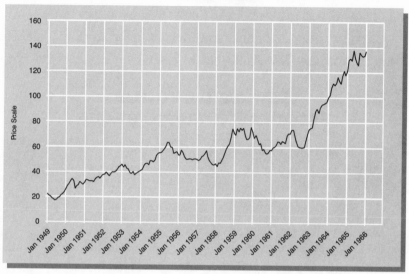

Though the designs were not so lavish, a similar boom occurred in the housing industry. Between 1945 and 1955, 15 million homes were built to provide the "good life" for young families. (The housing market got a special boost from a section of the GI bill that provided veterans with low cost mortgages.) Some 15 million housing units were constructed between 1945 and 1955, leading to historic highs in home ownership. And all of the businesses that served the housing market — tool makers, lumber, hardware, even the lawyers needed for contracts — thrived.

WATCHING THE TUBE		
Number of households with at least one set	Percentage with at least one set	Hours per day watching TV
1946 8,000	1%	N/A
1950 4 million	9%	4 hours
1960 46 million	87%	5.5 hours

With their homes built, Americans needed all kinds of consumer items to fill them. The appetite for appliances was almost insatiable. In 1946 just 8,000 American homes owned a TV. In 1950 it was 4 million. In 1956, Americans bought 20,000 televisions *per day.*

Of course, the TV boom was reflected in the stock market. The graph of Broadcast (TV/Radio) stock depicts a huge gain of 2095.5%.

STANDARD & POOR'S
BROADCAST TV/RADIO GROUP
1947–1966

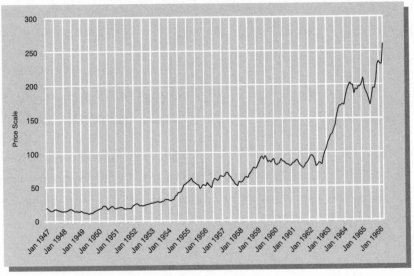

I was a pretty typical nine-year-old kid at that time. My family, which owned its home in the Bronx, didn't join the rush to the outer suburbs. My main interest was the New York Yankees, not the economy. But I did notice that my dad's business — trucking, warehousing, and machinery sales — boomed. He bought war-surplus chains, tools, and even machines like power winches, at rock-bottom prices and sold them retail for a good profit. Times were good for my family.

RAPID CHANGE

In the third mega-market, peace, new technologies like television, and low inflation and interest rates would stimulate a long running bull market. Not surprisingly, the stocks of broadcast companies would be among the darlings of the period. During the third mega-market this group would become the second best performer. But the rising tide would eventually lift almost all boats, and virtually every sector of the stock market would gain.

DOW INDUSTRIALS
1949–1953

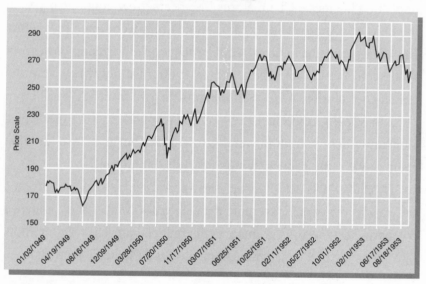

As we might expect, there is little evidence that anyone recognized that something as significant as a mega-market was developing. But people did understand that they were living in an age of rapid change and economic growth. Middle-class families could see it all in their daily lives. They moved to the suburbs, bought cars and appliances, and saw the development of a huge consumer marketplace. Enclosed shopping malls were built. Credit card buying spread as Diner's Club offered the first universal cards. (By 1960, Sears alone counted one in five households as cardholders.) And through television, mass market advertising stimulated enormous consumer demand. In 1956, the president of NBC declared that a higher standard of living had arisen because TV "has created an American frame of mind that wants more things, better things, and newer things."

If the 1920s was the era of the radio jingle, then the 1950s had to be the era of the television commercial. Scores of books have argued television's effect on society. We all have opinions on this, and all the other aspects of 1950s culture. But you cannot argue about TV's impact on business. Chain stores like Sears grew dramatically with the help of TV advertising, and brands that were once local, like Budweiser, became national. Money spent on advertising grew from $8 billion in 1955 to $12 billion in 1960. (TV networks were the main beneficiaries. At CBS alone, profits rose from $8.9 million in 1952 to $22.4 million in 1957.) People responded to the messages. Consumer debt, which powered growth like never before, grew at roughly the same pace, reaching nearly $200 billion.

Despite all this activity, many investors found it hard to envision a bull market that would last more than ten years. Many were frightened by sharp, short-term bear markets that popped up. They didn't know that one of the hallmarks of mega-markets is periodic corrections.

A DOUBLE BOTTOM STARTS THE THIRD MEGA-MARKET

Before the third mega-market began, stocks as measured by the Dow Jones Industrials reflected the shifting economy by making what we technicians call a double bottom. The Dow's first low and subsequent rally was a direct result of the end of World War II. The advance then faltered, as the first postwar recession took hold. This decline took the DJIA back to the previous low registered at the time the war ended. The retest of the Dow's 1945 low culminated in a double bottom. And it was this sequence (rally and successful retest of the previous low) that set the stage for the market that eventually carried the Dow to its postwar all-time intra-day high of 1001.11 in early 1966.

The outbreak of the Korean conflict in 1950 sustained the recovery by providing additional demand in the form of increased military spending. When the war ended in 1953 and that spending decreased, the economy entered its second postwar recession, but this, too, was mild and brief; by the end of 1954, the economy was recovering. That recession was discounted in advance by the Dow's decline, which began in January 1953 and ended in September 1953 (a loss of 13.8%). This sell off set the stage for another rally that lasted approximately two and a half years — a rise that foreshadowed the second postwar economic recovery.

DJIA & ADVANCE/DECLINE LINE
1949–1961

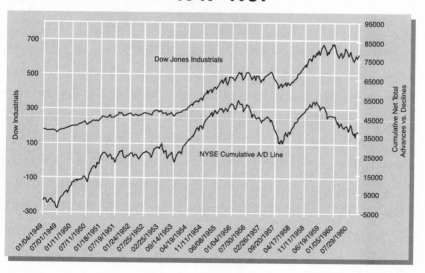

Stimulated by a boom in demand for consumer durables, the economy surged ahead in 1955. Record highs were made in the production of autos as well as in other consumer durables. As this boom collapsed, the slack was taken up by expansion in producer durables. The economy continued to expand until late 1957, as reflected in the graph of the Oils/Domestic Group shown below.

STANDARD & POOR'S
OILS/DOMESTIC GROUP
1947–1966

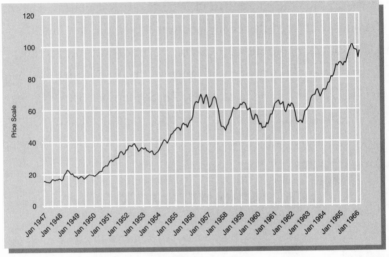

The third and most severe postwar recession came in 1957–1958. Once again, the Dow Jones Industrial Average, acting in its role as a discounting mechanism, peaked before the economy did and then dropped 20.4% between the months of July and October 1957. However, the broadness of this decline is captured more clearly by viewing the chart on the previous page of the Dow in relation to the NYSE Advance/Decline Line (A/D). This measurement of market breadth (A/D Line) peaked 16 months before the Dow peaked; hence, from beginning to end, the stock market, as measured by the A/D Line, declined for 19 months instead of only three months as measured by the Dow. The third postwar recession, therefore, had a much more severe impact on individual stocks than it had on most of the blue chip Dow components. Of a total of 46 Standard & Poor's sectors the average group dropped 15% during this sell off; the worst performer was Aluminum, down 53%, while the best performing group was Truckers, up 60%. Telephone utilities were typical of the market at that time.

TELEPHONE UTILITIES
1949–1966

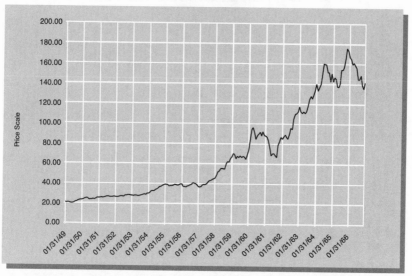

Another observation that I want to share with you regarding the action of the A/D Line is that the March 1956 peak was its zenith — this peak has never been exceeded. The March 1956 peak in the A/D Line was also the beginning of a major shift away from the Old Economy stocks of the day into the more "modern" or "New Economy" stocks of the 1950s and 1960s. And lastly, this A/D peak served as the beginning of the "footprint" of the third mega-market.

On a historical basis, the bear market of 1961–1962 was attributable in part to President Kennedy's showdown with Big Steel.

JFK had browbeaten unions into accepting modest wage hikes to cool inflation. After a contract was signed, the steel companies immediately jacked up prices. Infuriated, Kennedy demanded a rollback, and steel bent to his will. Stock prices were also affected by the Cuban Missile Crisis. Kennedy brought the nation to the brink of all-out nuclear war before the Soviet Union agreed to pull its atomic weapons out of Castro's domain.

DOW JONES INDUSTRIALS & NYSE ADVANCE/DECLINE LINE 1951–1966

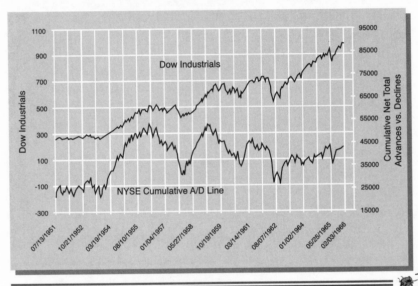

It's vital to recall that the period just after this dip was described by Ken Ward as the toughest market he ever saw. A great many investors jumped ship after the fourth correction. They, and most of the experts on Wall Street, could not recognize that a huge rally was in the offing.

I personally take delight in watching the stock market go up for what the so-called experts say is "no apparent reason." We have seen this during the current mega-market, and it happened in the third also. Consider these quotes from *The Wall Street Journal*, which were all published in the months after the missile crisis ended, as the Dow went on a tear, quickly gaining almost 20 percent and then a lot more.

"While stock prices recently have shown greater strength than in many months, market opinion among analysts remains mixed." (November 5, 1962)

"The Dow Jones Industrial Average posted its seventh sizable advance caused by no specific news." (November 8, 1962)

"Perhaps one of the best things about the current [market] psychology is that there are so many skeptics and so few real enthusiasts: such a general attitude often is insurance against any sharp decline in prices." (February 15, 1963)

The Wall Street Journal did not recognize that the fundamentals in the economy were so strong that a mega-market was inevitable. But as I've said, when bad news can't bring the market down, it's good news. The Cuban Missile Crisis was bad news indeed, but it was not the only bad news that the market was able to weather. A year later, when President Kennedy was assassinated, the market took an immediate 3 percent plunge. But when it became clear that President Johnson held firm control of the country and policy would not change, all of that loss was quickly recovered.

REASONS FOR ENTHUSIASM

During the third mega-market, Wall Street was all but immune to political events and the cultural turbulence that everyone envisions at the mention of the sixties. Every one of us who lived through it can recall the sexual revolution, the rebellion of the younger generation, and the incredible outpouring of creativity in the arts.

There were plenty of reasons to be enthusiastic about the economy. First, consumer demand was strong. Second, government on all levels had embarked on major spending programs — local roads, sewers and schools, interstate highways, the space race, atomic weapons development — that stimulated business across the country. And third, wonderful new technologies — computers, medicines, electronics — were maturing into powerful new businesses with amazing growth potential.

The space race, begun in earnest after the Russians launched *Sputnik* in 1957, put the government in alliance with business to develop new technologies. Six years later, huge electronics and aerospace companies had evolved in Los Angeles, the Pacific Northwest, and the Northeast. Typical was Raytheon (a Greek word meaning "ray from God") in Massachusetts, headed by a brash executive named Harold Geneen.

In 1956, when Geneen took over, Raytheon was heavily involved in making radar and missile parts — including semiconductors — for industry and the government. While profitable, this business was poorly managed and inefficient, and growth had been stagnant.

Raytheon also had a computer division that had never made a profit. In the competition to make and sell mainframe machines, IBM had beaten them at every turn. Geneen got them out of the race, selling his stake to his partners at the Honeywell Corporation. He focused the company on its core businesses, and in two years, Raytheon stock would more than triple.

Raytheon is a fascinating example of the kind of company that thrived in the third mega-market because it supplied the parts and technology that went into so many new electronic products. (In this way it was like Cisco today, which sells 80 percent of the routers and switchers that make the Internet work.) For Raytheon, it didn't matter which electronics company grew the most because it supplied all of them with parts.

THE CASE OF ITT

After turning around Raytheon and driving its stock to record highs, Geneen moved to a much bigger challenge, ITT (International Telephone and Telegraph). In 1960, ITT was very well positioned to profit both from new technology and the opening of the international marketplace to American companies. Decades earlier, after being shouldered aside in the United States by AT&T, ITT had established divisions worldwide to make telephone equipment, and, later, all sorts of electronic devices, from TVs in England to freezers in Scandinavia. But the firm had never been tightly managed and could not capitalize on its far-flung network of production and sales offices or on its access to advantages like low-cost labor. In fact, divisions in low-wage countries imported basic equipment from high-wage affiliates.

Geneen found duplication and mismanagement wherever he turned and responded by combining units and firing large numbers of workers. (In one infamous case, two subsidiaries serving exactly the same military clients occupied buildings that faced each other across a street in suburban New Jersey. These operations never communicated with each other and maintained almost identical lab and production facilities. Geneen put the two together and shed half the staff without losing any contracts.)

When he hired new managers, the dynamic Geneen tended to tap WWII veterans who had been educated under the GI bill and showed both worldliness and tenacity. In two years under Geneen's management, ITT's profits — mainly from foreign sales — rose by one third, and the stock price increased from \$14 to \$29. When the company reached \$1 billion in sales in 1962, the flamboyant Geneen had gold medals made and presented them to key executives. But he wasn't satisfied. He was about to focus almost exclusively on acquisitions, of any sort of company that would help ITT's bottom line grow.

It began with some small companies that were already in ITT's main line of work: telephone, radio, electronics. Then ITT began to look for large, established businesses that could generate profits as more-or-less freestanding companies. ITT would look especially hard for companies poised to grow much faster than their previous performance suggested. ITT became a pump maker, a radar manufacturer, and a major purveyor of heating and cooling equipment. With the purchase of Aetna Finance, the company became a consumer lender.

All of this activity baffled many people on Wall Street. They couldn't see that Geneen was assembling an altogether new kind of company: a conglomerate. His dream was to build a company so diverse that downturns in one business, or one country, would almost assuredly be balanced by improvements in another. But his aggressiveness inevitably brought him into conflict with other tycoons. In 1964 he bought a 10 percent stake in Comsat, the new company that would eventually handle all overseas telephone calls. He fought continually with David Sarnoff, still running RCA, over Comsat's pursuit of a monopoly. Geneen refused to agree to anything that would shut ITT out of any business.

Probably the most controversial of ITT's acquisitions was Avis, the car rental company. The Avis slogan — We're #2 but we try harder — surely explained why Geneen found the company so attractive. Though it was second in the market, behind Hertz, Avis nevertheless had a huge network and a recognizable name. All it needed was an infusion of cash and proper management to grow. In the first year after merging with ITT, Avis's earnings rose more than 30 percent.

Before the end of the mega bull-market, ITT's revenues exceeded $2.3 billion, and its stock passed $100 per share. Geneen had grown ITT into a business with 400,000 employees, 200,000 shareholders, and significant business operations in seventy countries.

But signs of trouble arose in 1966. A deal to buy the ABC television network failed. And unrest in Latin America threatened ITT's holdings there. Eventually, conglomerates like ITT would go out of fashion. And ITT itself was rocked by political scandal in the 1970s that drove its share price down to $35. Today it is a thoroughly reorganized company with a much narrower focus. But, during the third mega-market, it became a colossus, and it rewarded investors who recognized management's genius for growing revenues and profits.

THE DAWN OF THE COMPUTER

If ITT's run in the third mega-market is the story of one dynamic man's ability to ride a strong economy, the tale of the computer shows just how much value lies in breakthrough technologies. In the third mega-market, the computer industry was comparable to the automobile business of the 1920s. Many would try to cash in, but only a few would prevail. In the end, the determining factors would be an enthusiastic vision and an unwavering commitment.

Everyone knows that the first electronic computers were developed during World War II and used to aid the Manhattan Project. Many people thought of these machines as one-of-a-kind devices that would only be useful to scientists. After the war, American industry had to decide whether this new technology could ever be adapted for use by business.

Dozens of entrepreneurs believed in the computer's future and, just like the early car makers, started up shoestring companies with long-forgotten names like Alwac and Viatron. A lot of companies that had no real reason to believe they would succeed — Holley Carburator, General Mills — also gave it a run. All of these computer projects would disappear in the crush of competition.

IBM
1949–1966

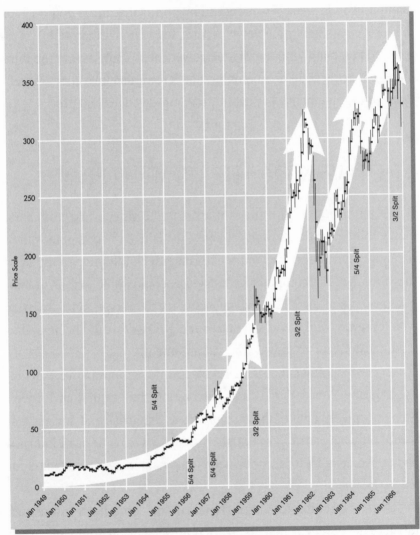

More notable were those companies that should have become big players in computers but lacked the vision or the commitment to do it. General Electric, which would be one of the most successful firms in the fourth mega-market, should have been in the forefront of the computer business. After all, it was a leader in electronics and possessed all the technological skill to develop computers.

But in the early 1950s, GE was led by a chairman, Philip Reed, who had seen the Great Depression and was extremely conservative. GE bought and used many early computers. In fact, it was the first commercial customer for a UNIVAC machine. But GE management doubted there would be much of a market for computers beyond huge government agencies and the 200 or so largest companies in the world. Instead of envisioning a mega-market, Reed actually feared another depression. Rather than invest millions of dollars in an exotic technology, he used GE revenue to pay down debt and prepare for hard times. When Reed retired in 1958, new managers at GE reversed his decision, but it was too little too late.

RCA was not so blind to the future of computers. In fact, the company funded major research into the technology. But David Sarnoff, still a radio man, could not envision his company as a major player. When the market for computers exploded in the late 1950s, the company would try to catch up. Like many, RCA would actually produce high quality machines. But it could not compete with the one firm that early on staked its fortune, and its future, on the computer: IBM.

Tom Watson, Jr., had been a WWII pilot and that may say something about the assertive approach he took to computers when he came to IBM after the war. (He quickly became president and would eventually take over as chairman after his father retired in 1956.) The company's profits had been stagnant for years, and Wall Street was hardly interested in its stock. Determined to make the company the dominant force in the computer age, Watson issued bonds to finance the development of an extensive line of machines. With each step in the development process, IBM consulted with its sales force and its customers to learn how to meet the needs of the market.

As with so many new industries, the winner in the computer race was not the company that was first to develop the superior technology. If that had been the case, Remington Rand would have swept away the competition with its UNIVAC. What made the difference for IBM was its far superior marketing force. In the decades leading up to the computer revolution, IBM had consistently rewarded its salespeople better than other office equipment companies. The company quickly fired poor performers, and those who remained were loyal. They hustled more and developed long-term relationships with their customers. (The superiority of IBM's salesmen was so well known that at business machine conventions competitors often wooed them with offers of big salaries and even envelopes stuffed with cash.)

When computers were new, many potential buyers were both excited and a little bit frightened by the technology. The last thing they wanted was a huge, expensive machine that they couldn't work. They trusted what IBM people told them, and Watson made sure that once machines were installed, the company provided the technical support to make them run.

Even though IBM sold machines that were slightly inferior to UNIVAC, superior marketing brought immediate results. Between 1952 and 1955, the firm's gross sales doubled, reaching more than $660 million. All the growth was in computers, as IBM grabbed 85 percent of the market. In this time, other companies actually raced ahead in technology. In 1958, while IBM still depended on bulky, hot-running vacuum tubes, Philco developed an all-transistor model that was faster and cheaper. But by then IBM had the cash flow and engineering prowess to make its own move to transistors and quickly caught up.

Mega-market conditions benefited IBM as higher wages increased demand for consumer goods and services. (In 1960, a communist bureaucrat visiting from Poland was shocked to see dock workers going to work in Cadillacs. As he saw it, American workers did not consider themselves part of a proletariat class but rather as capitalists in waiting.)

As demand for products and services grew throughout the period, industry looked for ways to become faster and more efficient. Often a computer was at the center of their strategy. One of the best examples involved our first case study company for the third mega-market, ITT. Determined to continually improve service, ITT's Avis car rental company was the first to computerize reservations. The Avis Wizard was an immediate hit with customers, and became a powerful cost-saving and marketing tool.

Though IBM was the clear winner in the new technology race, it was one company in a large sector that did amazingly well. The S&P Computers Hardware group was the best performer throughout the 1949 to 1966 mega-market, gaining an unbelievable 3206.9%. (This far outpaced the Dow's gain of 519%.) Many new companies found niches uncovered by the giant IBM and prospered. One good example was Control Data Corporation. Control Data was founded in 1957 and sought the high end of the market: laboratories and government agencies working on scientific projects. Because these customers already understood computers, Control Data could serve them without making a huge investment in training salespeople and support staff. For a brand-new company, Control Data enjoyed remarkable growth by avoiding direct confrontation with IBM. By 1965 it was number three in market share and number two in profit margin, at 12.2 percent.

Before that profit margin makes you too impressed with Control Data's management, consider IBM's numbers. In 1965, IBM owned

65.3 percent of the entire computer market, and it was selling as many machines overseas as all of its competitors put together. IBM's profit margin was a whopping 26.4 percent on revenues of nearly $2.5 billion.

By 1965, as IBM became the most dazzling stock around, it was clear to everyone that computers would be used throughout business and government and that the continual development of new generations of machines created an ever-expanding market. No one knew this better than the people on Wall Street. During the third mega-market, the volume of trading soared, as did the number of investors: 20 million new accounts were opened. Many of the more modern houses, such as Merrill Lynch, began to train brokers to serve investors as individuals. Others began distributing research to clients.

This was not the peak of public interest in stocks during the third mega-market. But throughout this great bull's run, everyday Americans often seemed obsessed with Wall Street. In 1959, *Life* magazine published a memorable article and series of photos from around the country that showed people poring over stock tables, staring at a "stock board" in a Merrill Lynch office, and even chalking up prices on a blackboard in a bar in Akron. That was their version of the televised stock ticker programs — CNBC, Bloomberg — that we see everywhere from restaurants to train stations today.

The third mega-market boom in stocks produced so much business that some Wall Street firms were overwhelmed by the volume of trading. Back offices had a terrible time keeping up. A total of 150 Wall Street firms closed their doors in the 1960s because back-office operations broke down so frequently that investors moved their money elsewhere.

Like all of the more sophisticated firms on the Street, Harris Upham and Co., where I worked, survived the crush of trading by turning to computers. We had a whole roomful of machines that

Market Frenzy in Akron

helped us keep up with the furious growth. I knew the computer could do more than office work, and I approached Mr. Henry Harris Sr. to ask if I could use the firm's massive IBM 360s. He arranged for me to have a couple of hours each week, beginning at 6 A.M. on Saturday.

This machine loved numbers, and I loved feeding them to it. I punched in support and resistance figures for 500 stocks, and way down at the other end of the room the printer would show me which stocks broke to the upside and which ones broke down. It was very exciting. One of the most exciting things was that we provided clean data. Most other houses had to put up with a lot of errors. And we got to make print-outs for our clients that were better than anything they had ever seen before.

(The only real problem with that first computer was the method you followed to enter data. It was the old punch-card system. They came in big trays, and God help you if, as I once did, you ever dropped the tray. I spent all of my allotted time on Saturday picking the cards up and putting them back in order.)

THE XEROX STORY

Although computers represented the most glamorous technology and IBM was a symbol of the third mega-market, its rise was not uninterrupted. At several points IBM took major hits, the worst coming during the market correction of 1962–1963. But overall the computer industry pulled the market in a positive direction. Other new technologies had a similar effect. Pharmaceuticals grew on breakthroughs such as the polio vaccine, and the arrival of jets made airlines a great performer.

But no discussion of this third mega-market would be complete without the story of the biggest business success of that time, Xerox.

The technology for the photocopier that would eventually be called a Xerox was discovered in 1938 by an obscure inventor named Chester Carlson who couldn't find a manufacturer to back it. He sold the rights to a nonprofit scientific institute called Battelle Memorial, which in turn licensed it to the Halloid Company in Rochester, New York. Hardly a corporate giant, Halloid literally went for broke, pouring $75 million into the idea. Executives and managers gave up their salaries and accepted stock instead just to keep the company going. Some even mortgaged their homes to support the copier project.

The Halloid Company approached this project with an obsessive zeal. Engineers were hired based on their energy and creativity. Subcontractors, who built most of the 1,200 parts in the first copier, were pushed to meet standards that were almost impossible. Management rallied the troops with constant reminders that they were part of an effort that would revolutionize offices and produce enormous financial returns for all.

The drama that surrounded the unveiling of the first machine was typical of the Xerox story. Invited to demonstrate their invention on live TV, the company shipped a machine to a New York station and its president went down to operate it. Hours before the broadcast technicians found a problem with the toner. Naturally, the only replacement available was back in Rochester. Fog kept the airplane carrying the stuff circling New York, but, with five minutes to spare, a messenger arrived with the package, and the demonstration went off without a hitch.

From 1960 to 1961, as photocopier sales began, Halloid's revenues went from $37 million to almost $60 million. A year later, the company's name was changed to Xerox. Expansion of the company's offices and manufacturing capabilities caused a boom around Rochester. A consortium of banks put up a $25 million line of credit for the firm, and alliances were made with foreign partners to sell Xerox machines worldwide.

In ten years, hundreds of people who had invested a few thousand dollars in Xerox became millionaires. Chester Carlson's profit from his invention exceeded $100 million, though he gave all but a tiny portion of it away.

THE PSYCHOLOGY OF THE MARKET

Xerox stock, which reached $171 a share, helped power the New York Stock Exchange on the final run-up of the third mega-market. It began on October 24, 1962, with the Dow at 549.65, and hit, on February 9, 1966, an intra-day reading of 1001.11. This was a gain of 82.1 percent in just under forty months. Among the forty-five Standard & Poor's groups, the average gain was 99.8 percent. Airlines, the number-one group, rose an amazing 578 percent.

But, as always happens in a mega-market, the sign that the party was coming to an end appeared well in advance of the peak. In May 1965 the Advance/Decline Line reached a lower high, the third since its zenith in March 1956. It once again gave the astute technician a lead time of about nine months before the Dow hit its peak.

This divergence is the continuation of my footprint, the pattern that all mega-markets follow, and it lasted for ten full years. During that period, investors shifted from Old Economy stocks to New Economy stocks, and the Dow Jones Industrial Average doubled. But I want everyone to know that negative breadth should be an early warning signal of a short to midterm Dow decline (corrections or severe bear markets) as it was in March 1956, March 1959, and May 1965.

If you were looking for other indicators to tell you that the mega-market was coming to a close, you could have found them in the psychology of the market. Remember from our discussion on Dow Theory that emotions lie behind most investment decisions. People enter the market fearing losses. When the bull starts to run they gain confidence. But ultimately they will get greedy. When that greed starts to set in, a correction is due.

In the mid 1960s, signs of greed were all around. One of the more obvious was the explosion in the number of mutual funds that were created and sold aggressively to middle-class Americans. As in the 1920s, salesmen actually went door-to-door signing up new accounts. Mutual funds were foolproof, they said, and many people believed. Many people bought without understanding the fees they would pay up front, and others were simply defrauded of their money by unscrupulous managers.

One of the most infamous of the mutual fund disasters took several years to unfold. It involved a California-based company called Equity Funding that sold people on both a mutual fund and insurance policies, which would be paid for out of the earnings of the mutual fund shares. Equity Funding turned around and sold the insurance policies on the secondary market, but ran into trouble when it was discovered that many of them were for sham clients. When the fraud was revealed, investors lost $300 million.

Investors also lost money on companies that bit off far more than they could chew in the acquisition game. The classic example was Ling-Temco-Vought, Inc., an electronics and missile manufacturing company. In 1958 when it began its buying spree, LTV was a small but profitable company with less than $7 million in sales. By 1969, it was a $3.7 billion-a-year giant staggering under nearly $2 billion in debt. The stock plummeted from a 1967 high of $169 to a 1970 low of $7.

Investors who jumped on the LTV bandwagon, or on the bandwagons of any of the high fliers, without checking the fundamentals, got burned when the mega-market ended. More cautious, some might

say more fortunate, investors did not suffer in this way in the years following 1966.

In fact, if you were in the market in 1966, and invested primarily
in stocks like IBM, Control Data, Xerox, Motorola, Polaroid, and others that were then part of what was called the "Nifty Fifty," you would
have continued to see big gains for years to come. They enjoyed major
gains until the Dow hit its final peak for the period in 1973.

In the period immediately following the third mega-market, science
and invention continued. The first jumbo jet was delivered in 1969,
and the floppy disk was unveiled in 1970. In 1971 the microproces-
sor would enter the computer scene and turbocharge the development
of ever faster and ever cheaper devices. The personal computer would
arrive a decade later.

These advances in technology were not enough, on their own, to
start a new mega-market. This is because the country lacked two of
the three major ingredients to support that kind of prosperity. Through
the early 1970s our peace was broken by the Vietnam War. When that
war ended we engaged in a very expensive period of Cold War, which
drained much of our ingenuity and energy. Finally, the feelings of
well-being that presage a mega-market were absent, too. Instead we
had oil embargoes, Watergate, the malaise of the Carter years, and
the recession of the early Reagan years.

Fortunately, the one constant in the market is change, and that
change is driven by the tides of history. No one could have foreseen
the revolution that was about to sweep the world. Fewer still could
have predicted just how it would happen, who would play the major
roles, and what the revolution would mean to the American economy.

CHAPTER 7

THE FOURTH MEGA-MARKET

THE YEARS AFTER THE THIRD MEGA-MARKET were long and frustrating for many investors. The Nifty Fifty, which I mentioned at the end of the previous chapter, performed well in the early 1970s. But as the decade continued, oil embargoes, Vietnam, Watergate, and inflation took their toll on them and on the whole market. The 1974–75 recession drove five million individual investors — about 15 percent of the total — out of the market entirely.

Double-digit inflation was a stock market killer, but it improved returns on many other investments. In the latter part of the decade, and into the early 1980s, millions of people invested in federally insured certificates of deposit that paid big returns. It was almost impossible to persuade them that stocks were the way to go.

To cool interest rates, President Carter appointed a six-foot seven-inch, cigar-chomping banker named Paul Volcker chairman of the Federal Reserve. His sole task would be bringing rates down. He chose to do it by tightening the supply of money, which had the immediate effect of actually sending rates higher. Mortgage rates spiraled past 18 percent. Businesses couldn't get financing. Volcker became the Darth Vader of the economy.

The pain Volcker created was real. Unable to finance new plants and equipment, thousands of manufacturing companies closed. Hundreds of thousands of people lost their jobs, and old manufacturing cities, especially in the North, suffered. Foreign competitors got the upper hand, and for much of the 1980s, America was known for making inferior goods. Nowhere was this more evident than in the car business, where the Japanese ate us for lunch.

At the worst, the prime rate reached 21.5 percent. Then a curious thing happened. Foreign investors began to see that U.S. bonds were a terrific investment, and they believed that Volcker would succeed in beating inflation. Long beaten down, the dollar climbed dramatically. This made foreign goods cheap, and stimulated an unexpected surge in consumer spending. Stocks began to recover, and by the summer of 1982 we were in for a strong bull market

On Wall Street there seemed to be no end to the number of companies that were undervalued and, therefore, terrific bargains. Many were bought out through leveraged buyouts, and transformed by the sale of divisions, layoffs, and new management. Leveraged buyouts (LBOs) are carried out with small cash payments and heavy financing, much like the purchase of a typical family home. Though a few disastrous LBOs got most of the publicity, most were successful. Companies improved their performance — through efficiency, shedding components, or better management — well enough to meet the loan payments. A few years later, when these same companies came back onto the market, they were leaner, more competitive, and often represented good value.

Unfortunately, investors who had waited a long time to see a bull market followed the path all the way to speculative frenzy. In August 1987 the Dow hit 2,700. This was a 300 percent increase in five years. But there were signs that warned of problems ahead. The Advance/Decline Line — the ratio of advancing stocks to decliners —

was showing that the great majority of stocks were not part of the rally. And in the broader economy, a soaring trade deficit and federal debt that seemed out of control made many people nervous.

Stocks began to lose momentum in the late summer. Then, in October, the worst one-day sell-off ever was precipitated by a crisis in the Middle East — Iran bombed an Iraqi oil tanker — that threatened worldwide oil supplies. The attack occurred on a Wednesday. America retaliated by bombing an Iranian oil platform over the weekend. As the market opened Monday morning the volume of sell orders was so huge that they simply overwhelmed the people and computers on the exchange. When this happens to a particular stock, the exchange suspends trading until the frenzy subsides a bit. On that Monday the selling mania was so strong off the bat many stocks didn't open until 10:30. By the end of the day, the market fell 23 percent on volume that exceeded 600 million shares, twice the previous record. In the week that followed, the companies listed on the New York Stock Exchange and the NASDAQ would lose half a trillion in value.

I remember that Monday — it's now called Black Monday — as the worst moment in my professional life. The 508-point drop was the largest one-day decline, in percentage terms, in history. People outside the business have a hard time picturing what goes on inside a brokerage house during an uncontrolled fall. In 1987, people walked around like zombies. Some were actually crying. Every few minutes someone would come into my office looking for some sort of encouragement, and I couldn't give it. I was like the captain of the *Titanic*, knowing it was going down and that there was nothing I could do. The only relief I felt that day came when an old priest friend called. He was worried about me. "You can always come back," he said. "You get three squares a day, a roof over your head, and free burial." We both laughed.

A couple of people claim they saw Black Monday coming. Maybe they did. I expected a correction, but nothing like what occurred. And by the time I saw what was really going on, it was too late to sell. We took it on the chin, like everyone else.

THE END OF THE COLD WAR

A lot of analysts and politicians looked at what was happening in the late 1980s and early 1990s and saw nothing but negatives. America was losing ground, especially to the Japanese, and might never regain its stature. Probably the worst symbolic moment of all came in 1992 when President Bush went to Japan, in part to beg for some concessions on trade. He ended up fainting at a banquet and vomiting into the Japanese prime minister's lap.

But when I look at the end of the 1980s and the early 1990s I see the beginning of the greatest surge of American business in history. The hard times of the 1980s were very painful, but they had also produced much tougher American companies. And once again, the stage was set by the conditions that must coalesce to produce a mega-market:

> The end of war and the dawn of peace
>
> New technologies
>
> Low inflation

About now you may be saying, "Wait a minute, Ralph. What war are you talking about?"

You are right. America wasn't on a battlefield anywhere in the world in the late 1980s. But we nevertheless won a huge victory and ended a long-running conflict. What did we win? The Cold War. It began back in the 1940s and cost us $6 trillion — invested in nuclear weapons, planes, ships, bases, you name it — in excess defense spending.

Because it took place in slow motion, the end of the Cold War is difficult to picture in our minds. In fact, much of what contributed to our victory was accomplished either in secret or incrementally. As a former seminarian, I see Pope John Paul II's aggressive moves toward Poland and other communist countries, which awakened popular democracy movements, as a major contributing factor. But make no mistake. The end of the Soviet Union didn't just liberate the citizens of the former Republic and the satellite states of Eastern Europe. It freed us from the burden of outspending the Communists, and thereby forcing them to keep up. The cost of this arms race was a major factor in the undoing of the USSR, but it also drained America of enormous amounts of capital and talent.

Think about it. For more than four decades a huge proportion of our nation's capital and our best scientists, engineers, and managers were devoted to the sole task of developing massively destructive weapons that we hoped would scare the Russians into submission. Trillions of dollars were spent making bombs and missiles that just sat in place, gathering dust.

Though Germany got to celebrate the dismantling of the Berlin Wall, here in America, there was no one moment to mark the end of the hostilities. But gradually, people began to agree that we could spend less on defense. Military budgets were cut back. And in Washington the politicians and bureaucrats talked of a "peace dividend," budget savings that could be used to reduce the national debt or fund tax cuts.

I was looking for a somewhat different dividend. The big payoff that comes with the end of war is not just a matter of dollars and cents. It comes, a few years after peace is declared, in the form of invention, enthusiasm, productivity, and a burst of growth as the people and technologies that once served the military are liberated in the marketplace.

AN OUTLANDISH PREDICTION

The fourth mega-market was preceded by what I called a "stealth" bear market. (I don't know who coined this term, but I'm pretty sure I made it popular.) The year 1994 was considered a corrective one because the Dow Industrials stayed within the confines of a 10 percent trading range and never broke below an important secondary low. At the same time, the transports and utilities went materially lower. I studied the chart of the Advance/Decline Line: I saw that more than 70 percent of the issues on the New York Stock Exchange actually lost over 20 percent of their value. When the majority of stocks perform in this manner and the Dow remains flat to slightly up — this is indeed a stealth bear market.

THE DOW JONES INDUSTRIALS WITH ITS 50- & 200-DAY MOVING AVERAGES 1994–APRIL 2000

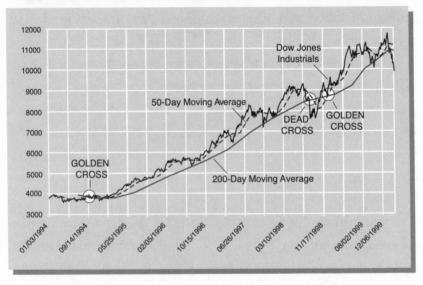

But after a long and frustrating wait, signs of a bullish trend finally emerged. You'll remember that in Chapter 3, I referred to the combination of 50-day and 200-day moving averages as an important trending tool. Used together they minimize the number of false Dow moves above and below the 200-day moving average. In the third quarter of 1994 the Dow Industrial's 50-day moving average crossed above its 200-day moving average. This was a "Golden Cross" buy signal.

At the same time, many of the general indicators I followed looked very good. Interest rates were coming down, utility stocks were picking up, and the S&P financial sector was rising. So while pessimists were predicting further market deterioration, I was seeing light at the end of the tunnel.

It began with what looked like an ordinary rally. From the first day of 1995, the Dow began climbing, almost in a straight line. Dow Theory signalled the start of the new primary bull market on February 23, 1995, when both the Dow Industrials and the Dow Transports closed above their previous important secondary highs. The Dow Industrials reached 4,003.33, well above their previous important secondary high of 3,978.36 registered on January 31, 1994. The Dow Transports went to 1,834.81, above the previous high of 1,596.85 registered on January 14, 1995.

With all of these indicators in place, my office sent out my 1995 stock market outlook calling for a target of a 500-point increase in the Dow. In the first half of the year, the DJIA went up 900 points! On Wall Street and in the media, other analysts described it as "unprecedented." *Investors Intelligence*, the keepers of the famous "sentiment indicator," which follows professional market letter writers, reported that the bears were consistently outnumbering the bulls. As a contrarian bull, I loved that.

The Street's low level of enthusiasm, despite a 900-point run, was yet another indicator that the bull market had more energy. Dow Theory — based on the industrials and transports — was positive. Interest rates were low. And key sectors of the market were all bullish. "Safe" companies like IBM were leading the breakout. But the gains made by these old reliable firms only represented the beginning of a more dramatic process. Even back in 1995, it was clear to me that the information superhighway, a phrase that predates the popularization of the word Internet, was going to be huge. This technology would usher in efficiencies that would rival the advances of the Industrial Revolution.

Technological development. History. The charts. Interest rates. They all told us that the economy was on the verge of being "born again." This was the moment when I finally wrote my Dow 7,000 report. In bold letters we announced, "the United States of America is on the verge of future greatness," and we spent sixty-four pages explaining why the Dow would go from 4,500 to 7,000 within three years.

Reaction was swift. Within days of the report going to our clients *The Wall Street Journal* published an entire article about it. They let me explain some of my reasons for making what seemed like an outlandish prediction.

On the Street, the report was music to the bulls' ears, but one individual attacked me ferociously, warning that technical analysis could not be used to predict long-term market trends — it's only a trading tool, he said. I could not have disagreed with him more. Fortunately, at 1 New York Plaza — Prudential headquarters — I had the backing of my bosses, and our clients overwhelmed us with more than 10,000 requests for copies of the report. But even up on the seventeenth floor, where I worked, I ran into critics. One colleague in particular told me, "You are going against consensus fundamental opinion." I replied, "Well then, whether I'm right or wrong, I won't have too much company." But then I always feel comfortable taking the unpopular side of an argument.

I didn't have much company, at first. In fact, the Dow took a 100-point one-day hit soon after my report was published and more than one of my colleagues asked if I had meant to predict Dow 700 instead of Dow 7,000. Fortunately, though, the number of advancing stocks was growing and I believed that the Dow, though it lagged, would climb too. I also expected that there would be plenty of dips along the way, but that the bull trend would dominate.

My original Dow 7,000 report warned that there would be several corrections, and they have indeed occurred throughout the fourth mega-market, many of them signaled by Dow Theory. The industrials and the transports peaked on May 22, 1996, at 5,778.00 and 2,296.20 respectively, and then a negative sell signal materialized in July 1996. A brief bear market followed.

However, another primary bull signal materialized when the industrials closed at an all-time high of 5,838.52 on September 13, 1996, and the transportation average closed above its previous secondary high of 2,057.62 that same day.

After hitting 7,000, the Dow remained in a trading range for a month or so and then turned down. It's interesting to note that the transportation average never followed suit. In fact, it held up well and scored another all-time new high soon thereafter. In hindsight, it was just a normal secondary correction for Dow Theory.

The primary bull market resumed, carrying the Dow Industrials to an all-time high of 8,020.77 on July 17, 1997. Between August 1997 and March 1998 the Dow became much more volatile while the transportation average remained relatively flat. Again, for the Dow theorists, this was a secondary correction, albeit a scary one.

On August 4, 1998, both averages broke below their respective important secondary lows and signaled a primary bear market. The industrials eventually scored a closing low of 7,539.07 on August 31, 1998, and the transportation average hit its closing low of 2,345.00 on October 8, 1998.

Although this is a matter of interpretation, I believe that the new primary bull market signal was given when, on November 2, 1998 at 2,954.85, the transports confirmed the industrials move above its important secondary high of 8,154.41 on October 15, 1998. The industrials eventually rallied to its January 14, 2000, closing high of 11,722.98 — an exciting bull run.

The true Dow theorist had to be concerned about this move over 11,000 because it was unconfirmed. In fact, the transportation index had actually peaked eight months before the industrials, on May 12, 1999. And guess what — we got another bear signal when the industrials confirmed the transports' negative bias on October 15, 1999, by closing below 10,019.71. Hence another primary bear signal was flashed and remains as I write this book. So far there have been ten noticeable rallies and ten subsequent declines. This roller-coaster ride began in November 1994, and many of these twists and turns were so rapid that I felt it important to detail some of them. In the next chapter, I will compare these reactions to those in previous mega-markets. But in the meantime, the ten rallies averaged a gain of +24.5 percent and lasted on average $4^1/2$ months. The best advance carried the Dow up 34.7 percent during the July 1996 to March 1997 period. On the ten declines, the Dow lost on average −10.8 percent and it took on average $1^1/2$ months to complete. The worst sell-off was a −20.8 percent loss suffered on the Dow between July and September 1998.

As I write this, the market is in another correction. Every business day, you can skim through *The Wall Street Journal*, turn on Bloomberg Radio, or glance at the CNN and CNBC market analysis shows, and find people talking about the "unprecedented market we find ourselves in." They question the wisdom of investing in "New Economy" stocks. They watch in amazement when these concept issues rise to huge over-valuations and are equally surprised when these same stocks reverse to the downside, washing away much of their overblown gains.

I wonder how much market history these critics have read. Wild price swings punctuated with periods of euphoria and despair are all part of a long-term bull market. These people don't understand that investors will periodically overstay their welcome (get greedy) and then be forced to disgorge these same issues (panic sets in). This is what I call the "psyche cycle" in the marketplace—the "greed-to-fear and fear-to-greed" syndrome.

But as we have seen in every mega-market, the new technologies, and the new ways of doing business — railroads, automobiles, or mainframe computers — have always been the place to put your money. As in the first three mega-markets, gains await in the companies that are either leading the revolution, or supplying the technology for it. Gains also await in the companies that are nimbly adapting and benefiting from it. Today, the stories of how two leaders, AOL and General Electric, powered the mega-market point to the bright future ahead. In GE's case, we can see that our success to date is not merely a function of new technology excitement. Old, traditional companies can take part in the revolution, and their presence makes the change even more profound.

THE RE-INVENTION OF GENERAL ELECTRIC

General Electric is the one company that has maintained its position as a component of the Dow Jones Industrial Average since its inception. GE has stayed strong for a century by adopting new technologies and growing into new areas of business, from electric power to appliances to heavy industry to finance. Sure, there were missteps (opting out of computers), but overall the company has thrived. Certainly it has enjoyed a remarkable run in this current mega-market.

In the early 1980s, GE was in the same boat with a lot of old-fashioned blue chip companies. Though it was a leader in some advanced businesses, like jet engines, most of GE's revenues came from old-fashioned manufacturing of electrical components, motors, and the like. Global competition was eating away at its base, and smaller, more nimble companies were exploiting innovations that should have come from GE. The company was losing market share in everything down to lightbulbs.

GENERAL ELECTRIC
1994–APRIL 2000

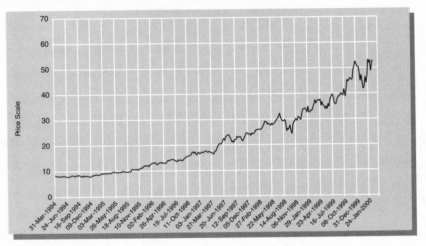

GE's new chief executive, Jack Welch, was horrified by the slow-moving bureaucracy that was to blame for many of the company's problems. Welch sold or closed more than one hundred GE businesses and cut the workforce by about 40 percent. He streamlined GE with a clear-eyed efficiency that caused some critics to call him "Neutron Jack," comparing him to a bomb that clears the people out of a business while leaving the building standing.

Most of the businesses that Welch abandoned were old-technology, or even no-technology activities like coal mining, oil refining, and housewares. He moved heavily into growth industries like medical technology, aerospace, and, with the acquisition of RCA and its NBC network, broadcasting.

One of the advances into medical technology was one of Welch's more brilliant moves. After meeting the head of one of France's largest technology companies at a tennis match, Welch suggested swapping the consumer electronics division at RCA — then a $25 billion-per-year business — for the French firm's X ray and medical imaging branch, which was then doing just $750 million a year. The French threw in $800 million cash and the deal was done.

Though the RCA consumer electronics business was huge in comparison, competition was fierce and profits were unreliable. Dumping it didn't cost GE much in earnings, and in the medical imaging business it gained a company with huge growth potential. It also played into Welch's plan to focus on global business, meeting competitors like Siemens and Toshiba head-on, not just in U.S.-based sales.

In those businesses that remained, Welch moved away from the hierarchical, military-style management that had ruled GE, and into a customer-oriented philosophy. He removed layers of middle management that stood between him and the factory floor. And he demanded that the managers who remained take more responsibility for their individual operations.

Though many people saw Welch as heavy-handed, he was actually trying to create a company that would require less top-down management, not more. His goal was a new type of workforce in which every employee understood GE's goals and would know how to achieve them. People who know where they are going and how to get there don't need much management.

Improving productivity became the mantra at GE. In part this was accomplished simply by convincing workers, especially in the older divisions that remained, that their jobs depended on their efforts. At the GE locomotive manufacturing plant in Erie, Pennsylvania, managers were brutally honest about business setbacks that forced layoffs. But when a big order for engines came in from China, the factory workers who remained raised their own hourly output to boost the company's margins and make their division more secure. One major contribution from shop-level workers was a spontaneous redesign of the engine cabs, which cut GE's costs dramatically. Instead of barely breaking even, GE made a good return on the train order.

A recent book by business writer Robert Slater, *Jack Welch and the GE Way,* detailed many instances where innovations from employees and new technologies were used to benefit both customers and the corporation. The lightbulb division revamped its billing system so that its computers could communicate with the biggest retailer in the world, Wal-Mart. The result was higher productivity, fewer mistakes, and gains for both companies.

Welch made these kinds of changes happen all over GE. It became a global leader in every one of its businesses. During the mega-bull market, the company's stock provided much of the muscle that moved the Dow. It stood near the top of every listing of the world's businesses, with a market value in excess of $240 billion.

One of the most remarkable things about General Electric's progress was that it was accomplished despite a few terrible problems. Its major appliance division was overwhelmed by a defect in its refrigerators. The division that managed the Hanford, Washington, nuclear weapons plant for the government was subjected to both environmentalist protests and a series of whistleblower lawsuits. And a billing scandal rocked the branch of the company that was making missiles for the Department of Defense. None of these problems made a real dent in GE's performance or its value.

THE STRENGTH OF THE BULL

When repeated bad news cannot bring down a company, you know you are looking at a winning stock. Likewise, when bad news cannot bring down a bullish trend in the stock market, you have a mega-bull in the offing.

As I pointed out in Chapter 1, in the mid-1990s, there was more than enough bad news for the bears to start to assert themselves. One of the most disturbing financial events was the Orange County, California, bond default. A sprawling, relatively wealthy community south of Los Angeles, Orange County was not the kind of place anyone would have associated with financial mismanagement. But the county lost $1.5 billion in bad investments and began to default on bond payments.

The second crisis that could have derailed the market was the Barings scandal. A young trader in the old British bank's Singapore office risked billions of dollars on the futures market and lost more than the bank's entire net worth. Venerable Barings was put out of business, after more than three centuries of serving kings, queens, and Europe's business elite.

The final dose of bad news came in 1995 from Mexico. Mexico's trade deficit had ballooned, and so had its borrowing. As investors began to notice that the government's cash reserves were being rapidly drawn down, they began to fear the Mexican currency would be devalued and moved their money out of the country. They were right. The peso collapsed and people holding Mexican government bonds lost billions of dollars. The government itself teetered on the edge of bankruptcy until the Clinton administration and the International Monetary Fund came through with more than $35 billion in loans.

Perhaps the most amazing thing about the Mexican crisis is that the country recovered very quickly. A cheap peso made Mexican goods very affordable, so exports skyrocketed. By 1997, all the loans had been paid off, and though inflation was high, so was growth.

For our purposes, it's important to remember that the Mexican crisis followed the outright collapse of a major international bank — Barings — and the shocking bond default by one of the richest communities in the country, Orange County. Through it all, the stock market refused to take a big plunge. It reached 7,000 in the beginning of 1997 and kept climbing to the year 2000 levels, above 10,000.

This doesn't mean that the fourth mega-market has escaped major corrections. As I write this, in the spring of 2000, a stubborn correction is underway. Other sharp corrections — a hallmark of mega-bulls — took place in 1996 and 1997. The Dow lost 500 points in October 1997, but it set the stage for a solid recovery, which took only five weeks to make back much of the drop. How long will the correction of 2000 take? That's impossible to say. But as I watch, investors are not cashing out but rotating their money into sectors they believe will be profitable. That tells me that this correction is simply wringing out the speculation, and preparing us to continue riding the mega-bull.

In my office at Prudential we have often reassured clients that these corrections were not killing the bull. In March 1998 we noted rather dramatic swings in the Dow Average and wrote: "Crazy, you say? We don't think so. These are the typical antics of the beast known as a secular trending bull market."

WELCOME TO THE INTERNET

I've mentioned the bad news that couldn't bring the fourth mega-market down. It's important also to recall the good news that has propelled the high-powered technology sector. In our original Dow 7,000 report and the updates that followed, we paid special attention to health care and the Internet. In the pharmaceutical area we recommended companies like Glaxo Wellcome and Bristol Myers Squibb.

It was a little more difficult to assess the Internet from an investor's point of view. For one thing, and I know that this is hard to believe in the year 2000, as recently as 1995 a great many people didn't believe that the Internet would become a household medium. At the time, connections to the Net were very slow, and the commercial systems built to serve the public were very unreliable.

Balky as the service could be, we looked at the Internet and saw amazing potential. To understand our view, you have to step back a little bit and take in the whole picture. The Internet was not a brand-new, untested technology. In fact, it had been up and running for decades. Its development began in the 1960s when the Department of Defense decided to link research computers at major scientific sites. Unbeknownst to the outside world, computers began talking to each other in 1965. From that moment, the network began to grow. E-mail was invented in 1972. The "domain name" system — all the .com and .net addresses we use today — appeared in 1983. In 1992, Congress and President Bush approved legislation opening the Internet to business and the general public. The Internet was going to be the biggest post–Cold War dividend of them all.

The potential of the Internet is obvious to everyone today. It is a vast system for connecting people that is as free for companies to use as the roads that link every city and town. The potential was enormous. The Internet could carry telephone conversations, orders from customers, and bids from suppliers. It could be a radio network or a television network. It could be the home for clubs or entire communities. People could pay their bills, participate in auctions, even write their own airline tickets.

On Wall Street in the mid-1990s we had to decide which corporations would benefit most from the growth of the Internet. Ultimately, a few of the companies that served as the public's link to the Internet — called ISPs, Internet Service Providers — would become huge successes. But the competition in this business would be ferocious. Early in the battle, the best bets had to be found in the infrastructure companies that made the computer systems that people would use to access the Internet and the companies that made the components of the Internet. Many of these companies were prominent in the list of buys we presented in our mid-1990s reports.

The classic example of an Internet infrastructure success was Cisco Systems, a California Bay Area company that was the primary supplier of routers, the devices that act like switchboards on the Net. Every company that wanted to play the Internet game — all those who would go on to be winners, as well as those who would be losers — needed to buy routers. (Just as the competing railroads of the 1880s needed steel and locomotives.) It was not difficult to see that the router business would make a good investment. In 1996 Cisco would sell $100 million worth of these things. In 1997, sales would be $3.2 billion.

In the mid-1990s, at the start of the fourth mega-market, the company called America Online was stumbling through a series of technical disasters and seemed destined to lose the competition with its better-funded rivals, Prodigy and CompuServe. Begun almost ten years earlier, AOL had been continually starved for the cash it needed to develop. No lesser figure than Bill Gates of Microsoft had declared the company a failure in waiting.

It's important to note that the man at the top of AOL, Steve Case, came from the world of business, not technology. In 1980, after college, he had gone to work for Procter & Gamble, a company known for its brilliant efforts to build consumer loyalty for its products. From there Case had moved to Kansas to work in middle management for Pizza Hut.

Case was an outwardly serene, but inwardly ambitious and curious young man. Bored and alone in Wichita, he bought a Kaypro personal computer and, with much effort, connected it to an early network service called the Source. By 1983 he had signed on as a consultant for the inventor of the Source, who was working on a plan to deliver video games, and later other services, via computer/telephone networks.

That first project, called Gameline, was a wonderful idea that was swamped by a downturn in the whole video game business, which had reached market saturation. But out of the debris that was Gameline's crash, rose the concept that Case and a few others would develop into an online service that included news, games, and chat. Called Q-Link, it went online in November 1985. On its first night of operations, it attracted exactly two dozen users.

With his background at P&G, Case was put in charge of marketing. In those early days he came up with the revolutionary idea of providing free software for the service. He created the name — America Online — in order to appeal to the broadest market. And after several stumbling attempts at partnerships with major companies — Apple, Commodore, Tandy — AOL chose to go it alone, through a public stock offering, in 1991. It had only 200,000 subscribers, compared with Prodigy's 1.75 million. But even then, Case believed AOL would dominate both media and online service in the years to come.

Case could be that confident because AOL was moving much more rapidly toward the future of the online world. Obsessed with providing what his customers wanted, Case continually made AOL easier to use and more pleasing to look at. And while Prodigy and CompuServe would focus on providing information and products, America Online would stress communication through e-mail, real-time chat, and clubs and groups that would span every imaginable interest area. Most of all, it was going to be mainstream, the McDonald's of the online world.

In the early to mid 1990s, the goal for every online service was to acquire as many subscribers as possible. In the very old-fashioned newspaper business, it's common simply to give the product away and hope that people like it enough to pay once the free ride is over. In 1993 AOL did pretty much the same thing. It began mailing disks to people's homes, tucking them in magazines, and even dropping them into cereal boxes.

The return on these mailings — meaning the number of people who actually signed on with the free disks — was an amazing 10 percent, and AOL began to grow. On Wall Street, the stock began to climb, from $75 in 1993 to $91.50 in 1994. It soon split, and then began to climb again.

AMERICA ONLINE
1994–APRIL 2000

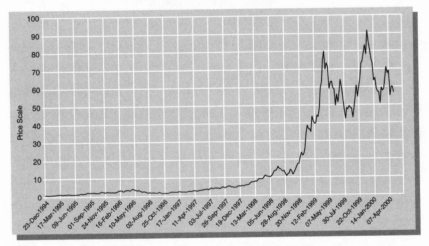

With the success of its marketing, AOL grew to nearly three million subscribers, becoming number one in its field in by 1995. There were problems along the way. The worst involved terrible traffic jams that meant that thousands of users couldn't access the service. At other times the system worked so slowly that customers could log on, go make a sandwich, and return without getting that familiar "Welcome!" from the service.

Fortunately, the company invested millions of dollars in making the service better, more user-friendly, and more attractive. It began to acquire software and communications companies that, once folded into the AOL recipe, lowered costs.

More challenges would follow. AOL would have to make the leap from being an online network — linking users to its own content — to being a true Internet provider, serving as an "on ramp" to the World Wide Web. A lot of outsiders thought this was impossible and wrote off AOL's future. But by this time the company was a name brand, almost as well known as Coke or Kleenex. AOL seized the Internet market and kept growing. In 1996, after several more splits, the value of the company's stock stood at $6.5 billion. Soon it would even acquire rival CompuServe's online business and its customers.

There have since been ups and downs. On occasions when investor psychology pushed the price down, AOL became a very good buy. Finally, in 1999, AOL pulled off the stunning takeover of media conglomerate Time Warner. With this move, it became a communications behemoth, well-positioned for the twenty-first century. Critics who had once said the company lacked interesting content, advertising sales potential, subscribers, or adequate growth were all silenced.

In the fourth mega-market the AOL saga stands as one of the most pleasing success stories. But a word of caution is in order here. In all mega-markets, the new technology — whether it's automobiles or radios or mainframe computers — produces competition that yields far more losers than winners. The second wave of the Internet gold rush has involved all sorts of companies that intend to use the new network to do everything from broadcasting TV-style programs to selling pornography.

A great many of these so-called dot-com companies offered stock and were bid-up by investors who were interested in anything that even sounded like it was connected with the Internet. A huge number of these companies were based on squishy business plans and never produced profits. During the periodic corrections that have taken place during the mega-market, these speculative stocks have been hit hardest. The way I see it, this is only logical. The market must wring out speculation and greed if it is to continue healthy growth. This is the same process we saw in previous mega-markets when poor performing railroads, auto companies, and computer projects failed.

UNDERLYING CONDITIONS

Five years into the fourth mega-market we have seen corrections and heard — at many different points — that it was all over. But there has not been a real change in the underlying conditions that produced the mega-market in the first place:

The peace dividend is still being paid. By 2003 the Navy will have 43 percent fewer ships than it did in 1989. The Air Force's fleet of small aircraft will be reduced by more than half. Partly as a result of decreased defense spending, government debt is being erased at a rapid pace. The post–Cold War peace is also bringing a benefit that was not so apparent during previous mega-markets — the expansion of global trade. The fall of Communism has opened huge new markets to capitalism, and American companies are moving in. And even where Communism still holds — China and Vietnam are key examples — trading has increased as local leaders succumb to popular pressure for more freedom and higher living standards. A significant recent development is China's pending admission to the World Trade Organization and the normalization of its trade status with the U.S.

Human capital is growing. All previous mega-markets have benefited from dramatic improvements in the quality of the workforce through education or immigration. The same thing is happening today. The world's best minds, whether from Ireland or India, continue to flock to America for opportunity. Today's worker is the best educated in history and is constantly upgrading his or her skills to adapt to changing technology. The enormous, permanent presence of women on the job has further broadened the supply and quality of workers. It has also added greatly to the growth potential of family incomes.

Technology continues to evolve. Beyond the Internet, science and engineering continue to give us amazing new discoveries and products at a rapid pace. Entire industries — cell phones, for example — are growing out of these developments and there are more to come.

Flexibility is breeding more creativity. The ability to change, whether it's a company moving into new technology or a worker acquiring new job skills, is the hallmark of this mega-market. Those who thrive in this era must be nimble. Fortunately, we all seem to have gotten the message. Workers today are no longer afraid of change. They are adapting and growing. The same is true for corporations. Even the very largest — General Electric is a good example — have found ways to be entrepreneurial.

Optimism. With no prospect of war and continued prosperity, America remains very optimistic. Despite the occasional correction in the market, investors continue to buy stocks. This trend should continue as the baby boomers move into the prime saving years of their lives and redouble their efforts to fund their retirement.

CORRECTIONS AND HEALTHY GAINS

In June 1997 I predicted that the Dow would reach 10,000 in about one year. Since we were trading below the 8,000 mark at the time, this was a very bullish pronouncement. Naturally we expected periodic corrections, bearish times when speculation and excess would be pruned from the market. "Because prices tend to spike up in an abnormal manner, they will also suffer sharp near-term sell-offs," I wrote. But overall we expected a kind of "buying panic" that would push the average up more than 20 percent.

At that time, the market had already met or exceeded the gains of the early 1960s, the era that had been the benchmark in my first report. I saw no reason for it to stop, and extended our time horizon past 2005. I also explained to Prudential's clients that I thought the bull was charging into a phase that would see gains broaden beyond the blue chips. I liked large cap stocks such as Sun Microsystems, mid-caps like Chris Craft, and small caps like John Nuveen. Within a year each of these stocks, and many in their sectors, went up by 25 percent or more.

But we didn't get to Dow 10,000 in 1998, as I had hoped. For the first time since the bull market began, I failed to meet my target. A very tough sell-off (actually a cyclical bear market in the third quarter) prevented it. However, I had not been caught by surprise. On August 4, I forewarned everyone of this impending decline. When one of the most exuberant bulls on Wall Street turns bearish, the media goes wild and the public reacts. My office filled with reporters and I trouped from one national TV show to another. I was accused of being the guy who single-handedly brought down the market. On that day, the Dow dropped 299 points. Some journalists called it Ralph's Tuesday. I told them all that I was still bullish for the long-term.

The recovery was faster than I expected. Of course, everything in the market — like the rest of the world — seems to happen faster today. News now reaches every investor almost instantaneously, and with the huge number of people now in the market, a change in sentiment can look like a stampede.

Dow 10,000 arrived in March 1999. Two months later it crossed the 11,000 mark. As I write this, we are in the middle of another dip, with the Dow off its peak and the NASDAQ, where more speculative high technology issues dominate, in a bearish correction. One major cause was the aggressive anti-inflation fight being waged by Alan Greenspan and the Fed. Repeated doses of higher interest rates scare the market.

I see a silver lining. Greenspan has been doing us a favor by controlling inflation and allowing the economy to grow at a comfortable pace, year after year. He is concerned that the "wealth effect" from the stock market's gains over the past several years is having a "negative" impact on the economy. Whenever the party gets too loud, he hollers at us all to quiet down — by raising rates — before the cops come and kick us out. This strategy has worked by squeezing down the overpriced stocks and cooling the economy, and it will allow us to return to healthy gains.

CHAPTER 8

WHY THE MEGA-BULL WILL
CONTINUE TO RUN

I MUST ADMIT THERE HAVE BEEN MANY TIMES when I have agonized over my assessment of the current mega-market. This is not a perfect science, and so many variables go into the creation of a mega-market that it is easy to imagine something going wrong.

And guess what. At this particular moment, as I am writing, I have been confronted with my biggest challenge. In April 2000 the stock market came under siege. The NASDAQ Composite dropped 29 percent in about fifteen trading days as investors panicked out of New Economy stocks such as biotech, Internet, and technology issues. Even prior to this, some technical problems had emerged. Dow Theory had flashed a major sell signal and the NYSE Advance/Decline Line continued its long-term downtrend.

I worried that the sudden shift in the stock market might have permanently altered the course of sector leadership. And just as I did before completing my Dow 7000 report in early 1995, I reflected on the huge risk that I took by writing this book. The immediate future appeared less bright. What would happen to my credibility if the entire market soured?

But then I reminded myself of the central themes in this book. I asked myself a series of questions to discover if any of the major tenets of the mega-bull market concept had been negated as a result of the market's rapid descent.

Is the United States threatened by a major war?

The answer is no. Our nation is basically secure. The peace dividend continues to be paid. By 2001, four rounds of base realignments and closures will have reduced the domestic military basing structure by about 20 percent from its 1988 level.

If you want to get an on-the-ground look at the positive effects of reduced military spending, take a look at the communities where bases have been closed. In almost all of them, civic leaders fought the closures tooth and nail because they were afraid of going without Uncle Sam's dollars: Unemployment would rise; businesses would close; grass would grow on Main Street. In fact, the opposite has happened. In many of these military towns, old bases have become sites for economic growth. Of the sixty-two communities that have faced major base closures, about two thirds have unemployment rates equal to or lower than the national average. Almost two thirds of them have growth rates higher than the national average. And, if past experience is any indicator, as time passes and they have more opportunities to adjust, many of the others will grow, too.

Is our economy about to embark upon runaway inflation?

Here again, the answer is no. There are no serious signs of inflation, and Alan Greenspan and the Federal Reserve have been vigilantly easing interest rates up to squeeze out any potentially inflationary factors.

Greenspan's concern that the "wealth effect" from the stock market's gains over the past several years is having a negative impact on the economy is well-founded. In early 2000 there were signs of "irrational" behavior on the part of the gang who day trade. His rate hikes have periodically scared this segment of the market, creating brief mini-bear markets that eliminate the excesses.

Did the baby boom generation disappear?

No. Even the sharp decline in April 2000 could not totally discourage them from putting money into the stock market. Their 401(k) plans remain, but they are shifting or rotating funds between sectors, and this is what keeps the mega-bull market alive.

Did the technology revolution stop dead in its tracks?

No. Some biotech- and Internet-related stocks did break sharply to the downside early in the second quarter of the new millennium. But the young, talented people in Silicon Valley are still hard at work. New discoveries in medicine and advances in computer and Internet technologies are continuing.

Have the trends established by the four-year market and presidential cycles changed?

No. The current mega-market actually began with a four-year market low in November 1994. The prior four-year low was registered in October 1990, measured by the DJIA. By extrapolating this four-year series out in time, we see that another important market bottom was made on August 31, 1998 (the Dow's closing low of 7,539.07). If history is any guide, then the next major lows should come in 2002, 2006, 2010, etc. The presidential cycle, discussed in

Chapter 2, fits neatly within this pattern. Upon being elected in November, the incoming president should theoretically enjoy a "honeymoon rally" that could last several months and could even carry into his second year in office. Then we usually see a meaningful decline. That sell-off (or bear market) usually ends with a four-year-cycle low. During the last two years of a presidential term, the market usually works its way higher. The third year is usually the strongest. How this trend played out in the last decade is shown.

MARKET CYCLE & PRESIDENTIAL CYCLE FROM 1990–APRIL 2000

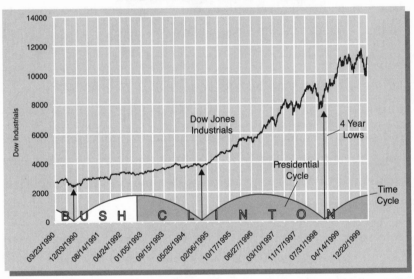

It's not enough for me to *tell* you that the tenets of technical analysis indicate that the mega bull is still with us. There are plenty of bearish professionals and academics who would disagree, and I will deal with some of their arguments.

Most of these bears base their arguments on one or both of two factors: the negative Advance/Decline numbers or the high P/E ratios of many stocks, but especially those of new technology companies.

THE NEGATIVE ADVANCE/DECLINE LINE

Let's take a look at the A/D Line argument. It is true, as I write, that the NYSE Advance/Decline Line has suffered significantly versus the DJIA, after peaking on April 3, 1998. More stocks are in retreat than are charging ahead. But they will not end the bull market. In fact, negative breadth — which is what we call this situation — is an integral part of mega-markets past and present. This is because a great many companies are lagging behind the growth stocks that are leading. However some of those laggards will eventually re-invent themselves and join the advance. This is the natural ebb and flow of a mega-market. And it explains for me why the persistent negative breadth is less ominous in the long term than the big bears believe.

Not convinced? Then consider that there have been other periods when breadth lagged the Dow for greater lengths of time without terminating the mega-market. During the third mega-market, for example, the A/D Line peaked and trended lower for twenty-three months (see graph on next page). During that period the Dow suffered three noticeable declines: 11.5 percent between April and May 1956; 10.4 percent between August and October 1956; 20 percent between July and October 1957.

The important thing to notice is that after the declines, a very powerful advance resumed. Even so, the A/D Line failed to register a new high like the Dow. In fact, the A/D Line has never been able to better its March 1956 high. And yet the Dow continued its mega-market by doubling over the next ten years

In three out of the four mega-markets (we have no figures for 1877–1891) the A/D Line has descended even as the Dow has risen. These divergent trend lines, which I now refer to as the "footprint" of a mega-bull market, are problematic for the short to intermediate

term, but are not deemed critical for the longer term. They reflect a
movement away from the mundane companies of the day to the leading
firms of the period. The successful firms are usually the large capitalization stocks — many are in the Dow list — that are the leaders of
the era. This will be true today. It is these stocks, along with the growth
issues, that will dominate throughout the life of a mega-market.

DOW JONES INDUSTRIALS VS. NYSE ADVANCE/DECLINE LINE JUNE 1955 TO AUGUST 1959

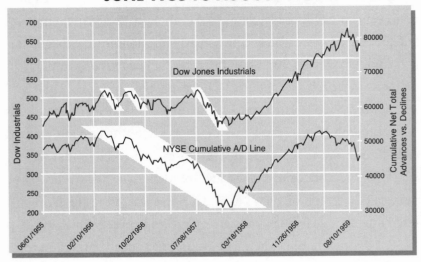

P/E RATIOS

Now let's address the second factor that the more gloomy observers all
cite to support their claim that the sky is falling — P/E ratios. Simply
put, a P/E ratio is the price (P) investors pay for $1 of a company's
earnings (E). A stock that costs $10 and has $1 per share in annual
earnings has a P/E ratio of 10. A stock that costs $100 and has earn-
ings of $2 has a P/E of 50.

Many experts look at the history of P/E ratios going all the way back to the founding of the New York Stock Exchange and see that, on average, stocks have cost around $14 per $1 of earnings. Every time the average P/E gets too high, it is knocked down. (Quants refer to this as reverting to the mean.) And since the current market has the highest P/E ratios in history, they are absolutely convinced that a big knock-down is coming.

But as we've seen before, no one measure is enough to give us a real understanding of the market. And in this case, when you examine the larger companies that are the backbone of the economy, you see a much different picture. Among the 1,100 largest-cap companies in the U.S., more than half of them have P/E ratios below 20. If you take the technology stocks out of the entire group, their average P/E is an amazingly low 12.1.

This closer look at P/E ratios reassures us that just a few high fliers in the technology sector are skewing the average. And there are many investors who believe that the potential growth for these companies is so great that they are worth high P/E multiples. Whether you agree with them or not, it's clear that in the rest of the market, there are many good values and there is much more room for growth.

But before we leave the P/E controversy, to reassure you further, let's consider this analysis by one of my colleagues, Ed Keon, who is the head quant at our company. Ed maintains that in the old days, investors really focused on earnings and dividends. John D. Rockefeller said he was only happy when he got his dividend checks, and everyone else had the same attitude. They didn't trust company directors to hold on to money or invest it in growth. They wanted their quarterly checks. At the same time, the growth in earnings or share prices meant little. And in the first half of the twentieth century, growth averaged just 3 percent.

After World War II, earnings and stock prices began to grow in value at a much healthier rate. Responsible corporate officers were expected to invest in new technology and in expanding their markets. Values rose. The trend picked up steam to the point where earnings growth has averaged better than 7 percent a year since World War II, and it is not unreasonable to expect that in many years it will exceed 10 percent.

Now, if investors were willing to pay a P/E of 14 for 3 percent growth in a company's earnings, wouldn't it make sense that they would pay a lot more, say a P/E of 28, for double that level of growth? When you look at it this way, today's P/E ratios are not at all unreasonable.

To make the picture even brighter, Ed Keon reminds us that American companies have the potential for even greater gains as the world marketplace opens itself to real competition. We learned the lessons of the 1970s well: Our plants are more efficient; our technology is the absolute best; our products are the highest in quality; and most firms have only begun to reach out to the rest of the globe for sales. Even among the top twenty S&P stocks, many have foreign sales that are below 30 percent of their gross. Untold numbers of quality American companies have zero foreign sales. Because of peace, the growth potential for foreign sales, given the competitive advantages of the United States, is phenomenal.

THREE SCENARIOS

How phenomenal? The answer is suggested by our previous experiences with such extraordinary times. I've developed three scenarios — call them great, greater, and greatest — for the years ahead. Each is based on a previous mega-market.

MEGA-MARKET ONE SCENARIO

There is still plenty of time left for today's market to mirror the gains of the first mega-market, which racked up a 280 percent gain on the

Cowles All Stock Index. In fact, the Dow has already advanced 225 percent and so all that is necessary now is a DJIA rally of another 2002.62 points above its January 14, 2000, high of 11,722.98.

Such an advance would match the 280 percent gain registered by the Cowles between 1877 and 1891. Since it took $14^1/2$ years to complete the first mega-market, it means that, theoretically, the Dow Industrials could reach 13,725.60 by the year 2009. I think that such a target is attainable, but I think we can do better.

MEGA-MARKET TWO SCENARIO

It is conceivable that today's Dow could rise a full 496.5 percent, as it did between 1921 and 1929. However, there is a time constraint when it comes to matching this scenario perfectly. In this current mega-market the Dow has already used up $5^1/2$ years just to garner a gain of 225 percent (November 1994 to January 2000). Thus, in order for the DJIA to mirror the second mega-market in both price gains and in time, it has to hustle to attain an objective of 21,545.58 by the middle of the year 2003. I think that this scenario is unlikely due to the lack of time, but not due to the lack of the market's potential.

MEGA-MARKET THREE SCENARIO

I see this as the most likely scenario because the current Dow has more than enough time (seventeen years) to complete its task of rallying a total of 518.9 percent from its November 23, 1994, low of 3,612. Such a move results in a potential objective of Dow 22,354.67 by the year 2011. I don't think that too many people would find this an unreasonable expectation. It gives enough leeway for the stock market to have a couple of normally flat years and even a few anticipated bear markets before reaching this lofty goal.

THE MARKET AS A WHOLE

It is one thing to use the popular Dow Jones Industrial Average as a yardstick for the stock market but at some point we must broaden our gauges to look at all the sectors and groups that make up this thing called the stock market. Sector analysis suggests that many groups have even greater upside potential than the Dow Jones Industrial Average.

Consider the ten best-performing sectors measured from their 1994 lows to the highs they achieved in either 1999 or early 2000. The list starts with the absolute best gainer, Electronics — Instrumentation, up 1803.7 percent during that period.

Group	% Gain	Year of its High
Electronics — Instrumentation	1803.7	2000
Biotechnology	1568.7	2000
Computer Software/Service	1309.7	2000
Electronic — Semiconductor	1230.2	2000
Telecommunication (Wireless)	1163.8	2000
Computer Networking	969.2	2000
High Tech Composite	946.1	2000
Electronic Defense	903.9	1999
Computer Hardware	878.2	2000
Investment Banking/Brokerage	793.4	1999

These groups represent the technology of the day. However, they are the most volatile. If you play these sectors, you need to have the stomach for considerable swings, which could be opportunities for successful market timers. In the long run I see no reason why they shouldn't be among the sectors that will continue to lead the fourth mega-market.

On the second page of this book I gave a negative answer to the question: "Why am I writing this book?" I stated that my primary goal was to find out why the stock market looked to me like it could still go much higher. I was not concerned then, nor am I now, about capturing newspaper headlines with a big futuristic Dow target. I know everyone wants a huge number and a far-away date, but they will just have to wait a little longer, because my answer will only come about by process of elimination.

Earlier on in this chapter, I stated that my biggest challenge in writing this book surfaced when the market came "under siege" in April 2000. I then stopped myself and began slowly eliminating any doubts concerning the awesome appetite that the baby boom generation still had for investing and put the fears of rising interest rates and runaway inflation into a more realistic perspective. I also reassured myself that American technology and its resultant impact on productivity were not short-term phenomena. And lastly, I reiterated my belief that democracy's triumph over Communism has set the stage for a more peaceful world, a world safe from total conflagration.

AVERAGE RALLIES DURING MEGA-MARKETS

Period	% Gained	Duration
First Mega-Market	40.2	16 months
Second Mega-Market	18.3	$3^1/2$ months
Third Mega-Market	38.6	16 months
Fourth Mega-Market	24.5	$4^1/2$ months

Peace does not mean total calm in the markets. In fact, history reveals that volatility is a big part of every mega-market regardless of whether the bull began running after the Civil War in the late 1800s or greeted the twenty-first century with record highs in the late 1900s. The statistics I gleaned while researching all four mega-markets reveal that their respective rallies and declines were more or less similar in percent performance and length of time, as the tables above and below illustrate.

AVERAGE DECLINES DURING MEGA-MARKETS

Period	% Lost	Duration
First Mega-Market	−12.7	10 months
Second Mega-Market	−8.9	1 month
Third Mega-Market	−17.3	6 months
Fourth Mega-Market	−10.8	$1^1/_2$ months

PHILADELPHIA SEMICONDUCTOR INDEX— RELATIVE PERFORMANCE TO THE S&P 500 1994–APRIL 2000

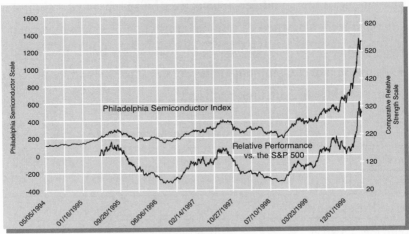

Volatility can also be seen in key sectors of the market, but it does not end the mega-bull's run. An example of just how an important sector in today's mega-market can come into and out of favor and yet not derail the mega-market's overall major trend is seen in the activity of the Philadelphia Semiconductor (SOX) Index since 1994.

Note that starting in September 1995 the SOX Index not only dropped about 50 percent in price over the next twelve months but dramatically underperformed the market (S&P 500). The same thing happened a second time, between the middle of 1997 until October 1998, when the SOX suffered another 50 percent loss with devastatingly poor relative performance, and yet the mega-bull market survived.

I think most investors forget that a bull market, or in this case, a mega-market, does not live on one group or sector alone. The secret to success is "rotation" — the ability of investors to move from an overvalued (or as the technicians might say, overbought) situation(s) to undervalued (or oversold) groups and sectors. This rotational activity enables money to stay in the stock market and not be forced to chase only overextended situations.

Bear markets within a mega bull are also be to expected and are not fatal. Drops of close to, or more than, 20 percent did materialize during each mega-market, as shown below.

BEAR MARKETS WITHIN MEGA-BULL MARKETS	
Period	**% Lost**
First Mega-Market (1877–91):	
September 1882 to June 1884	−22.3*
Second Mega-Market (1921–29):	
May 1921 to June 1921	−18.7
March 1923 to July 1923	−17.5
Third Mega-Market (1949–66)	
July 1957 to October 1957	−20.4
November 1961 to June 1962	−29.2
Fourth Mega-Market (1994–2011)	
July 1998 to September 1998	−20.8**

* *This percent is based on the performance of the Cowles All Stock Index.*

** *This mega-market began in November 1994 and has already enjoyed five successive years of double-digit gains. The odds now favor a few flat to down years before the market continues with another string of yearly back-to-back gains.*

With all of the history in place, from a bullish peace environment to hair-raising volatility, the profile of the mega-market is complete. But in any market there will be better and worse places to put your money. In the next chapter, I'll point you in the direction I think is best and answer the questions about the market that I'm most frequently asked.

CHAPTER 9

MORE PROMISE THAN PERIL

E ACH AND EVERY DOLLAR put in the stock market is both an investment in a company and an investment in America's future. Like our country, the market offers us both promise (growth and prosperity) and peril (the possibility of loss). By now I hope you share my hope and enthusiasm for both America and the market. My optimism is based on the fact that the conditions for our fourth mega-market remain in place.

The post–Cold War peace holds. In fact, the freedom movement that began in Eastern Europe in the 1980s is rippling out to other countries. Even China is opening up. This will be a huge new market for American business.

Inflation and interest rates remain in check. The Federal Reserve seems to have developed the capacity to dampen growth before the economy gets too overheated. This has happened several times now, and it has allowed us to continue with growth and prosperity while avoiding inflation and recession.

New technologies continue to roll out of labs and research centers. The Internet is getting faster and bigger every day. Experts believe that by 2005, the number of people online will surpass 1.7 billion, a fourfold increase over today. This is just one of the areas where innovation flourishes. But it is one technology that will accelerate all the others, and bring all of humanity closer together. The effects on business will be astounding. To understand much of what the future holds in e-business, I turned to my colleague at Prudential, Nick Heymann. What follows is a vision of the future that he and I share.

THE E-BUSINESS REVOLUTION

A shakeout, the likes of which has never been seen (both in terms of its scope and warp-speed pace), is now unfolding in industrial America and with its competitors around the world. What I am talking about is the conversion to an e-business (electronic/Internet business) model. This will be a do-or-die kind of challenge, as it is unlikely that companies who fail to convert will be acquired but rather they will be "hollowed out" because their ability to create shareholder value will have long since disappeared. At the risk of oversimplifying a complex system, the following comprise several of the most critical components, processes, and virtual spaces required to operate an e-business system:

- **Back office.** Establishing global supply-chain alliances and fully integrating them with an extranet, which is an external network that allows suppliers and channel partners, among others, through a company's firewalls, and provides access to proprietary information. The new lingo for this type of activity is Business to Business (B2B).

- **Front office.** Determining optimal ways to meet customer needs; developing customer Web interfaces that seamlessly link with alliance partners offering related products and services to best meet customer needs. This modern business practice is called Business to Consumer (B2C).

- **E-hubs.** Joining or ideally establishing leading e-hubs or "virtual markets" that, because of their incredible scope of products and services offered by almost all manufacturers and service companies in the served market, become the industry's dominant virtual exchange.

- **"Electronic backbone."** Electronically interconnecting and integrating all virtual constituencies of a company's served market (suppliers, customers, Web interfaces, and e-hubs) via an "electronic fiber channel backbone" that can exchange massive amounts of data on a real-time basis and enable a company to operate in realtime as an e-business.

(Just as a point of clarification, however, I want to distinguish between two often discussed e-business strategies: business-to-business [B2B] and business-to-consumer [B2C]. B2B typically refers to the trade of raw materials and/or finished goods and services that are incorporated into products and services resold to an end consumer [i.e., through retailers]. Looked at another way, B2B e-commerce is trade between a company and what are generally considered its business partners [on both the back-end and front-end], not individual consumers. On the other hand, B2C e-commerce generally refers to online retailing, including the sale of products and services and provision of information, and focuses on selling finished goods generally to individual consumers [you and me]. B2C companies must focus on and understand traditional retailing concepts such as merchandising, store design [Web layout], marketing, and advertising to entice the end consumer.)

The new millennium brings with it the "e-contenders" versus the "e-pretenders." It is pay-off time for those companies that "get it," those companies that are doing everything to convert as rapidly as possible to an e-business model so they can flourish (rather than perish) in the new economy. As in the past three mega-markets, there will be survivors and there will be those who fail because they did not understand how, refused, or simply did not move fast enough to reinvent themselves and their companies.

Again, I must take you back into history for a little perspective, but, may I add, I don't have to go back very far to explain the mega changes that are happening in the world of e-commerce. After the end of the Cold War and the dismantling of the Berlin Wall, the world economies increasingly embraced capitalism as the de facto standard for sustained viable growth in commerce; global expansion replaced regional dominance as the primary source of expanding demand and revenues and earnings for most traditional "Old Economy" companies. In essence, all that was required to succeed was the ability to provide the same goods and services on a global basis better than competitors. This ushered in a period of growth for traditional global multinationals throughout the 1990s.

Today, it's the global Internet that has become the defining factor in shifting where value is added. With the Internet forming a reliable, instantaneous global interconnected communication structure, a company's physical presence has been displaced by virtual presence. The result is that those companies now deemed to possess the strongest growth prospects typically provide either electronic technology or intellectual capital, not physical products as we have known for the past century or more. No longer will providing the best-quality "physical" product be adequate to sustain historical levels of value creation.

Traditional companies currently are also finding their brands no longer give them the right to raise prices. Instead, value (as measured in terms of enhanced functionality rather than just outstanding quality or the lowest price) is what consumers demand from any product or service they choose. In the future, simplicity and speed will be valued by consumers far more than endless features or enhancements. With the advent of wholesale clubs and global buying alliances, the pricing dominance of leading branded product companies is now meeting its match. Consumers, not producers, are enjoying a shift in the balance of power within virtually all market segments, whether consumer or industrial.

Of course, I can understand the logic of why companies would want to lay out carefully their plan of attack in preparing to convert to an e-business model. But given the "need for speed," if any conversion attempt is to deliver its maximum potential payback, time to plan simply isn't a luxury that can be enjoyed in this process. They must just go for it.

For potential investors, the following are the keys to understanding the e-business dynamic:

- You must comprehend why and how e-business is virtually redefining the historical business model.
- Recognize that those companies that do not already possess at least a clear understanding of how they plan to convert to an e-business model will face tenuous fundamental prospects very soon.
- Realize that the current division between Old Economy and New Economy companies is not set in stone. While not all companies will prevail, strong rationale exists that at least a handful of the industry's best managed and positioned companies will prevail in the New Economy.
- Understand that timing of implementation will prove the most critical determinant to successful implementation and conversion to an e-business model.
- Grasp that it is unlikely that there will be any "safety nets" to fall back on should a company fail to rapidly convert.

To find an example of an old dominant company that has moved successfully into e-business, I can turn again to GE. E-business is pervasive in every aspect of General Electric's operations. Every business in the GE family conducts customer transactions via the Internet. Web sites provide extensive autonomous solutions and problem resolution capabilities, which, in addition to transaction capability, typically offer GE's customers such things as ordering customization, remote monitoring of orders currently in production, efficiency diagnostics for existing installed base equipment, as well as performance comparisons with similar products or services among peer group companies. Of course, GE cross-sells its various products across all businesses, offering to help finance, insure, or resell products.

What readily distinguishes GE's e-commerce initiatives is that the company's already high intellectual content is actually in many ways significantly enhanced through various programs and features incorporated into GE's Web site customer interfaces. Not only do most contain highly specialized software and wireless technology that allow for remote monitoring and efficiency testing, customization allows customers to modify their order to better meet their needs as well as access and resource other GE products and services from separate businesses that they might not have been aware existed, which could also help meet their needs. When you see Old Economy companies "get it," put them in your portfolio.

THE NEW AGE OF RETAIL, OR SHOULD I SAY E-TAIL?

While e-business describes a sea change in the way large companies are interacting with customers, most of us will be more affected by the technology revolution in more ordinary ways in our daily routine.

Whether we are purchasing sporting equipment or sending flowers, the way we buy and sell all kinds of goods and services will never be the same.

In this new era, just about everything is changing positively for the consumer. First, online retailers are offering us greater convenience, and wider variety in items as diverse as books, CDs, toys, and travel. But the advantage doesn't stop with convenience. Online retailers are offering lower prices, more information at the point of purchase, and personalized shopping experiences to all of us wherever we live and at any hour of the day or night.

Even though there are still many uncertainties about this online revolution, there are clear characteristics that we can look at that will determine who will survive in this industry. The winners must all create three important outcomes:

- They must attract consumer traffic.
- They must convert the browsers to buyers.
- They must sell merchandise or services without giving away the "store."

Without these three elements, a retailer, whether online or not, doesn't have a chance to survive. So far, one major e-tailer — eBay — stands out as a potential winner; eBay best characterizes "The New Age of Retail" because its entire process is end-to-end digital (although sellers still must physically ship a product), while its large community of buyers and sellers allows for tremendous growth and economies of scale. It is estimated that $5 billion of gross merchandise sales will be transacted through the eBay marketplace in 2000, and eBay is likely to increase the size of its market exponentially. Regional auctions allow eBay to expand into product categories such as used furniture, real estate, used autos, and event tickets, which are unsuitable for national or international auction markets.

Many people believe that the online distribution channel will eventually allow product manufacturers to cut the middleman out of the value chain. Dell Computer, with its consumer-direct business model, is perhaps the most successful example of this trend. However, this kind of direct selling will likely only work in certain industries, such as PC hardware or autos. In these industries, only a few brands exist, and consumers are far more likely to know which brand they want prior to purchase. Yet, in other industries, such as travel, apparel, or recorded music, consumers prefer choice, and I believe that retailers as multi-brand intermediaries are in the best position to offer choice to the consumer.

The ultimate question for businesses involved in e-tailing will be: Who owns the consumer? Product manufacturers will try to gain direct access to the end consumer, while online retailers will try to win consumer loyalty through multi-brand product offerings and value-added services.

The competition will be decided, of course, by consumers, who are likely to be armed with an ultimate weapon: smart software. Also known as "shopping bots," smart software could change the shape of retail forever. Shopping bots, working on behalf of the consumer, gather information and negotiate a transaction without human intervention, based on consumer preferences.

An investor who considers the e-tailing future naturally wants to know which retailers will be the ultimate beneficiaries of online commerce. While pure online retailers such as Amazon.com, eToys, and Webvan are blazing trails in the online marketplace, each will face serious competitive challenges from traditional retailers, as those brick-and-mortar stores shift focus to the online distribution channel.

Again, we can look to mega-market history. The railroads helped create a consumer shift to mail-order goods in the nineteenth century. This made the growth of huge new catalog retailers like Montgomery Ward and Sears Roebuck & Co. In the first mega-market the entrenched retail stores missed an incredible opportunity, and allowed start-ups to control the new marketplace. It is not yet clear whether retail giants today will make similar mistakes. But it is certain that some will make the leap and be strong investments.

THE DATA INFRASTRUCTURE

Both e-tailing and e-business require a basic infrastructure — networking, Internet service, data transmission systems — to function. Think of it as a new kind of transportation network that is now growing like topsy in an environment where deregulation has increased both competition and innovation.

Not long ago, data moved in a trickle from one site to another. You could spend half an hour waiting for a few pages of text. Today, new technologies emerge almost on a weekly basis, making communication practically instantaneous. The demand for this service is enormous, and the companies that serve the marketplace have amazing growth potential. Many are familiar names — Nortel, Cisco, Lucent, Tellabs — but there will no doubt be newcomers, and the market will favor some over others.

What's more important to understand is that this is a massive new industry that is developing a technology that is far from mature. Consider the airplane. It took decades for the Wrights' invention to be transformed from a novelty to a mail carrier to a planet-shrinking marvel. Right now the data industry is in the mail-carrier stage and has a long way to grow.

THE BIOTECH BREAKTHROUGH

History teaches that scientific discoveries can produce revolutions in society. Since the 1700s, these kinds of breakthroughs have been made roughly once per century. In the 1700s, it was the discovery of a smallpox vaccine that began a 200-year decline in what was once the scourge of humanity. In the 1800s, it was pasteurization. In the twentieth century, the first major breakthrough in basic medicine was Alexander Fleming's discovery, in 1928, of penicillin. Even today, drugs that descend from Fleming's discovery save lives around the world.

Fortunately, the end of the twentieth century saw the end of the one-in-one-hundred years pattern for medical revolutions. Science has been accelerated to the point where advances are made at a dizzying rate. Leading the way is the biotechnology industry and its affiliated laboratories and scientists.

The modern biotechnology industry can be traced to humulin, a drug that was developed by Genentech less than twenty years ago. Since then, more than 120 biotech drugs have been approved by the Food and Drug Administration, and nearly 450 new ones are in clinical trials, with a record number in advanced clinical trials.

To understand the potential profits for investors, it helps to look at a single one of the new drugs, Genentech's clot-buster Activase. Given at the onset of chest pains, Activase breaks up coronary clots, allowing the flow of blood to be restored to the heart muscle and limiting damage. When Activase was first approved for use in 1987, there were no drug treatments available for the 1.3 million Americans who suffer heart attacks every year.

With Activase's arrival, cardiovascular medicine changed. Intervention became the watchword, and new devices were invented to protect patients from heart attacks. Balloon angioplasty, in which catheters are used to open a narrowing in a coronary artery, was invented and became widely used.

Stents, miniature coiled springs, were invented to be placed into the diseased section of the coronary arteries to keep them open.

Though saving lives has been the main priority, these medical advances have also created wonderful new businesses. Activase sales in 1999 were $236 million, while total angioplasty catheter sales exceeded $1 billion, and stent sales were $2.1 billion.

The industry spurred by Activase is just one of many to come. In the coming years, biotechnology will produce great numbers of new drugs that will extend the human lifespan, reduce the need for costly hospital procedures and long-term care, and dramatically improve the quality of our lives. It is not inconceivable, to me, that the average person will soon be able to look forward to a ninety- or one-hundred-year-plus lifespan with many more active years beyond today's retirement benchmark age of sixty-five.

And this is just the beginning. With the advent of the human genome project — which is mapping the entire human DNA package — biotech has been energized by the possibility of gene therapies for inherited diseases, cancer, infectious disease, and cardiovascular disease. Genetic research is also contributing to the development of new kinds of vaccines, which promise to work against existing diseases, such as cancer.

Taken together the biotech areas — gene therapy, vaccines, and more conventional pharmaceuticals — promise a wonderful future for humanity and for the investor. It is one area I expect will provide direction and continued energy for the fourth mega-market.

MORE TECHNOLOGY GAINS

Along with the obvious areas ripe for technological innovation — computers and the Internet — I believe the immediate future holds dramatic improvements in unexpected sectors:

Transportation will, I believe, be revolutionized by hybrid vehicles that will use much less energy than today's cars and trucks. Some will utilize fuels other than gas. Many will have both electric and combustion engines, which will both power the car or truck and recharge its fuel cells. Lighter, stronger materials will produce even greater efficiencies, and the cost of transporting both people and goods will fall.

Food production will be radically improved by genetic engineering. I know that this is a controversial issue in much of Europe, but genetically altered foods are already on our tables and fear will be overcome as concerns about environmental safety are resolved. Along the way, we will get more abundant crops that are grown with fewer pesticides, are easier to ship and process, and are much less likely to spoil.

Environmental concern will lead to more efficient communities and manufacturing industries, and to new products made with recycled materials. All over the world, governments and business are creating new types of housing, mass transit, and industrial processes that use less energy and other natural resources. This development also creates jobs, adding more people to the ranks of customers for American exports.

FINAL QUESTIONS AND ANSWERS

Everyone wants to ask a stock analyst questions. We're something like doctors in that we often wind up doling out free advice at every social event we attend. In light of the market at the dawn of the twenty-first century, and all that we have explored together, I'd like to leave you with the answers to some of the questions you might ask if we found ourselves side-by-side at a dinner table or cocktail party. They review, in capsule form, some of the main points in this book.

QUESTION: *Why did you start this long-term bullish book with a bearish warning?*

ANSWER: Let me begin by repeating the warning I made very early in the Foreword of this book: All bull markets, including the mega-markets I am writing about, undergo sharp drops along their way to a peak. Such periodic washouts are common and are necessary for a mega-market to be sustainable over the long term.

Technical analysis, if used correctly, should help identify both bullish and bearish markets. I hope I've convinced you to take advantage of its usefulness and to apply its theories and basic tenets to timing your stock purchases and sales.

QUESTION: *You wrote that previous mega-markets have quite a few positive traits in common. Are there any disturbing, negative similarities?*

ANSWER: Yes, there are a few similarities that are problematic. Let me start with the obvious one, sentiment. Without a doubt, investors got too carried away with their fast profits during this market's explosive rise between the October 1998 low and the first quarter of 2000 high. They piled into small biotech stocks, unknown dot-com issues, Internet companies, and others. An air of hysteria characterized the market. Even the novice technician could identify the trend as irrational and not sustainable. To say that some of these stocks will not rally even halfway back to their lofty highs is being kind.

A second and most disturbing element is the problem of breadth in a mega-market. Both the NYSE and OTC advance/decline lines dropped precipitously during the frenzied rally mentioned above. Unfortunately, these lines represent the direction of all stocks on their respective exchanges; thus, the majority of issues never enjoyed what, on the surface, appeared to be an exciting bull market. In Chapter 3, I referred to the divergence between the Dow Jones Industrial average and the A/D line as a "stealth bear market."

DOW INDUSTRIALS & NYSE ADVANCE/DECLINE LINE 1994–APRIL 2000

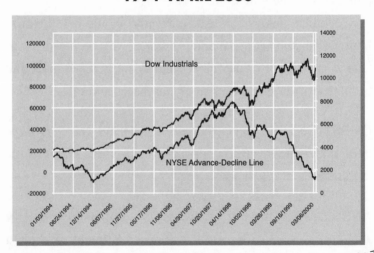

QUESTION: *It sounds like you just described the end of a mega-market. Is that where we are in the fall of 2000?*

ANSWER: I don't think that I described the end of a mega-market. In fact, the long-term divergence between the Dow and the NYSE Advance/Decline Line (breadth of the market) is not unusual in a mega-market. As you read in Chapter 7, this disparate trend lasted ten years during the third mega-market before any serious sell-off occurred in the DJIA. I still expect this kind of long-term divergent activity to continue because in mega-markets it is the new technology (New Economy) of the era that will dominate over time, and this dominant leadership will manifest itself as the split in stock participation continues.

Over the lifetime of a mega-bull market, growth and technology stocks will lead. Of course, there will be periods where leadership will revert to value and to the small and mid-size capitalization stocks. It is this ebb and flow between these leaders that makes market timing so invaluable. Rotation is the life line of every mega-market.

QUESTION: *Can you explain the sell-off in high-tech and Internet stocks in the spring of 2000?*

ANSWER: To help answer this question, I must share with you a conversation I had early in 2000 with Arthur Levitt, head of the Securities and Exchange Commission. I asked him what his thoughts were regarding the hectic and speculative pace of day trading by the fearless "pump-and-dump" crowd in the chat rooms on the Internet.

In a priestly voice he simply stated, "Ralph, the market will teach them a lesson."

Within weeks, the market indeed turned against this fast crowd. And I welcomed the severe drubbing endured by the high multiple (ridiculously overvalued) stocks. The smug confidence of some of these day traders had to be reined in. The market is not an arena for gambling. Good old-fashioned investing with proven fundamentals must be the order of the day, not some hot tip begotten by "word of mouse."

QUESTION: *Why do you insist that today's mega-market began at the bottom in 1994? What about starting at the low in 1982?*

ANSWER: I get this question quite often because most students of the stock market know that the up-leg that finally took the Dow above its historic 1,000 barrier began in August 1982. Hence for many individuals the market's modern-day major uptrend began at this low point.

I agree that 1982 is a very significant point in the market. However, as you read in my previous chapters, I believe *peace* is the primary driving force behind the entire mega-market. And this major change in our country's thrust actually happened when the Berlin Wall came down in November 1989. For me the world as we know it had a new starting point. And as in the previous post-war mega-markets, it took several years (until late 1994) before the reality of true peace set in and the market commenced its advance in earnest.

QUESTION: *Aren't you worried about the increasing public interest in the stock market?*

ANSWER: In a word, no! First of all, the public is tied to the fortunes of Wall Street more today than at any other time in history. People have good reason to be attentive to what is going on in the financial community because of their involvement in IRAs and 401(k) plans. They need the information, and the popular business TV shows are educating them.

QUESTION: *What would make you bearish and negate your mega-bull market scenario?*

ANSWER: The primary consideration would have to be another serious war. The Persian Gulf War and the problems in Kosovo are not the same as WWI or WWII or for that matter Korea or Vietnam.

Yes, there are trouble spots but they tend to pose a general threat and not just to the United States. For example, India and Pakistan have made ominous noises at each other and a conflict there raises the specter of nuclear war. But Japan and nations in the region have a strong interest in not seeing this happen. Thus the likelihood of a large-scale conflict is minimized by the realization of what it would cost and the fact that so many countries would be negatively affected.

QUESTION: *Could the fourth mega-market end in a crash like 1929?*

ANSWER: One of the significant contributing factors to the Crash of 1929 was the overextension of margin credit. This means that people were able to buy stock with little cash and finance the rest of the purchase using the stock as collateral. As stock prices fall, their collateral loses value and people have to either come up with more cash or sell out their stock holdings (that's a margin call). That in turn increases the selling pressure, and a downturn becomes a free fall.

Lessons were learned from 1929, and from subsequent downturns in the market. As a result, margin credit has been tightened. Stock sales and mutual funds are closely regulated. Program trading limits have been imposed. That is not to say that risk does not still exist or that the market is devoid of speculation. But I do not expect the Great Crash to ever be repeated.

QUESTION: *What about the prospects for inflation in the next few years, and won't that derail the mega-market as it has done for others in the past?*

ANSWER: One thing that is important to remember is that we've learned from past mistakes. Economists have different views about the causes of inflation. If you read the papers, you see that inflation is caused by an overheated economy; what that means is that there is too much demand and that tends to cause prices to rise. The analogy is an auction with people bidding against one another for, say, a painting or a piece of memorabilia. If a number of people want the item (too much demand) the bid will go up. This is basically what happens in the overall economy too; lots of people with lots of money to spend bid up prices overall.

However, you will also read about "supply side" factors in inflation, for example the increase in oil prices that follows production cutbacks by OPEC. If the price of oil and its derived products increases, prices of other goods go up to incorporate the rise in business costs.

While economists may disagree about some of the causes of inflation, there is much more consensus about the role played by the supply of money and by interest rates. During the fourth mega-market, the Fed has been especially adept at balancing rates and the money supply to keep inflation in check. I expect this to continue under Fed Chairman Alan Greenspan.

QUESTION: *Well, maybe Alan Greenspan has this in hand, but what about his successor? How many more terms is Greenspan likely to serve?*

ANSWER: History again teaches us lessons here; Greenspan's predecessor, Paul Volcker, had to deal with the high inflation of the late 1970s. He had tremendous global credibility as an inflation fighter and everyone wondered who could possibly replace him! But clearly Alan Greenspan has done an excellent job and is credited by many with steering the economy along its present path. While no obvious successor seems to be apparent, it is likely that whoever succeeds Greenspan will have the same overall goals of keeping inflation down and promoting the health of the economy.

QUESTION: *What happens when the baby boomers all start retiring and pulling their money out of the market? Shouldn't that start happening in 2006?*

ANSWER: All baby boomers are not going to pull out all of their holdings at once. Most financial advisors suggest that people change the profile of their portfolios in stages as they get older, which should minimize a sudden shift. Moreover, many people will have incomes that will permit them to continue to be invested in the market even as they are starting to draw on their retirement savings. Congress just recently removed the earnings ceiling on Social Security, which will enable older workers who so desire to continue to work without losing their benefits. This additional income will moderate the drawing down of holdings. Moreover, coming behind the baby boomers is the "echo" generation that will be increasing their investments, particularly as they reach the middle years of a typical life span. So overall there will be an influence on the market, but I think it will come about gradually and not in one sharp sell-off.

CONCLUSION

I believe that history and the insights provided by serious technical analysis offer support for my view of the current stock market. We are in the middle of a true mega-market, and it could well promise a much longer run.

But remember, the stock market is not just dry statistics and hot money. It is really people. Our study of the mega-markets, from first to fourth, proved that. Markets are driven by human desires for profit and growth, and by emotions ranging from hope to fear.

Because the market is human, and all things human are somewhat unpredictable, you must use technical analysis and every other bit of information you can find to support your investment decisions. Sure, we can forecast a general trend, but we will be surprised from time to time. Markets never move simply in a straight line, point A to point B. The only way to cope with the inevitable surprises is to be prepared.

I don't think it is an accident that we are experiencing the longest business/economic cycle in our country's history. Most people forget that Europe is currently enjoying the longest stretch of peace (55 years and counting) since the Holy Roman Empire. In the words of General Colin Powell, "I would be very surprised if another Iraq occurred. . . .

Think hard about it, I'm running out of demons. I'm running out of villains. I'm down to Castro and Kim Il Sung" (April 1991 in testimony before Congress). I believe that there is an irrefutable link between peace and prosperity, and *that* is the theme of this book.

My final thought is embodied in a word I would like to coin: *Ameriglobe*. For me it means the "Americanization of the globe." When the Berlin Wall fell, it signaled the triumph of capitalism over Communism. As a result, the American system of doing business is being adopted around the world. For example, six out of the ten largest corporations in Australia are run by Americans. A little area outside of Tokyo, known as "Bitter Valley" (renamed "Byte Valley") is turning into the Japanese version of our Silicon Valley. Here young graduates are able independently to create ideas and new companies outside of Japan's normally rigid business system. This sounds more like individualized American thinking than the traditional Japanese way of doing things.

In Europe, it is almost a daily occurrence to read about another huge merger or acquisition — even hostile ones like in the U.S. Again, not the traditional way of doing business. There are no more national boundaries; the world is up for grabs as corporations globally reinvent themselves.

Individual investors around the world are also being Americanized. Our popular business/TV shows are a big part of their daily lives. The CNN, CNBC, Bloomberg shows, etc., have had a huge impact on their attitudes. Typically, Europeans were bond buyers, but today the percent of equities in their portfolios is increasing partly due to their exposure to these equity-oriented shows. And over time, the Chinese, who are natural risk-takers, will become more capitalistic — at least they will create their own version. This can't be bad for democracy and peace around the world.

Remember, peace is bullish. And you can't separate humanity's bright future from its financial future.

ACKNOWLEDGMENTS

B EING A FIRST TIME AUTHOR is very exciting. However, if it were not for my family, business friends, and acquaintances, this entire process would have been a veritable nightmare. I cannot thank them enough for their encouragement, their insight, and their invaluable data.

I must begin by thanking the two people who started this project with me and supported it without restraint; they are professors at my old alma mater, Iona College, in New Rochelle, New York: Ms. Mary Lesser, Ph.D., Associate Professor Economics, and Brother James T. Carroll, C.F.C., Ph.D., Assistant Professor of History. Together they weaved a tapestry of economics and American history, which served as the backdrop for this book.

James Dunnigan, an author of sixteen books, was the third person who rounded out my theme by adding his expert knowledge on military history. My firm, Prudential Securities Incorporated, totally supported all of my efforts and understood when I had to temper my travel schedule: Hardwick Simmons, CEO and President; Michael Shea, Executive Vice-President, Director of Global Equity Research; Theodore Smarz, first Vice-President, Director of Equity Research Administration; Dennis Drescher, Executive Vice-President, Director of Private Client Advisory Services; Richard Franchella, Senior Vice-President, National Sales Manager; Charles

Perkins, Senior Vice-President, Director of Public Affairs and Susan Atran, first Vice-President, Public Affairs; John Driscoll, Vice-President, Capital Markets Coordinator; David Basich, Vice-President and Mutual Fund/Annuity Coordinator; Cecelia Haggerty, Project Manager; and William Chettle, our Creative Director. In our legal department: Steven Bard, first Vice-President, Director of Marketing Review, and Nikki Procopio, first Vice-President, Associate General Counsel.

Market data was provided by John C. Brooks, of Yelton Fiscal, Inc., and Paul F. Desmond of Lowry's Reports, Inc. Group statistics came from the fine people at the Standard and Poor's Company. Many of the stock charts were provided by Bridge Information Systems. And the creation and digital reproduction of all these charts was done by The Graphic Source Inc. — Ira Geringer, Alvoris Hood, Jeremy Cummins, Joe Dretto, Adam Estabrook, Dado Lam, Angel Calle, and Stephen White.

My nephew Gregory Woods jump-started this book by poring over mountains of data from Bryan Taylor, Global Financial Data, and from the Alfred Cowles III and Associates' book, *Common-Stock Indexes*. Shelley Lebeck, of the Market Technicians Association, opened the doors to their library, allowing me to peruse their impressive collection of technical books and articles.

Kay Logan untiringly typed the original draft and patiently listened while I grumbled about it. Thanks, too, to my fellow analysts at Prudential Securities who offered their research and time so that I could better understand and write about their respective industries: Peter Drake, Ph.D., helped me in the biotechnology area; Nicholas Heymann, Senior Consumer Electrical & Electrical Equipment Analyst and his team — Mohammed Ali, Rory Cohen, and Igor Maryasis — gave me invaluable insight into the e-business revolution; Mark Rowen guided me in the e-tailing industry; and John Butler, Vice-President, and his team — Geoffrey N. Hansen and Jess Lubert — shared their thoughts concerning Optical Networking Systems and Components. And Edward F. Keon, Jr., Senior Vice-President, Director of Quantitative Research at Prudential Securities, and his team — Tara G. Stergis, Jamie A. Coleton, Joshua Friedlander, and Gloria M. Ramirez — offered insights into the question of valuation.

Danielle Hudson, my secretary and my "boss," quietly agonized with me over the many real and imagined fears that I had about this project. Phil Choremi forced the computer to make charts that seemed impossible to create. Peter Martin carefully scrutinized the manuscript. The people in the copy center printed many manuscripts for distribution: Harry Morales, Christopher Williams, and Adrian Seabrook. My Bostonian friend, Bill Doane, Minuteman Financial Services, Inc., turned his personal technical library upside down in search of old graphics. My buddy in Florida, Walter Deemer, Deemer Technical Research Inc., directed me to some old books for popular quotes and stories about famous old personages in the field of technical analysis.

Robin Griffiths supplied me with the history of technical analysis in England. Rosemary and Thomas Sherlock provided the B.R.A.C. report which shed light on current military base closings; and Eileen Walters did the follow-up research concerning military downsizing.

Peter Cooper, from my old Kidder Peabody days, impressed me so much with his quote: "The most fundamental thing about a company is the price of its stock." My cousin Tony Acampora provided me with a European perspective from Geneva, Switzerland. Michael D'Antonio came to my rescue during the final weeks of writing my manuscript and neatly pulled the whole book together. Takanori Hiramoto has always enjoyed sharing the fascinating differences between the wonderful peoples of Japan and America. Paul Brown initially guided me in the writing of my manuscript. Brian DeFiore, my agent, made this all happen. The folks at Hyperion were helpful, enthusiastic, and professional, starting with Will Schwalbe, Executive Editor; Bob Miller, Managing Director; Martha Levin, Publisher; Ellen Archer, Marketing Director; and Michael Burkin, Sales Director. Fernanda and Sotos Yannopoulos helped me with the Italian wording in my dedication.

Thanks to you all.

And, of course, my thanks beyond words to the most patient group of all, my family: Marguerite Acampora, Edith A. Woods, John and Diane Acampora, Jay and Chris Woods, Tess Woods, Tanya, Greg, and little Emily Woods. They all waited patiently for the day that the manuscript would finally be completed so Uncle could be free again.

THE STATISTICS FOR THE FOUR MEGA-MARKETS

Performance	Cowles 1877-1891	DJIA 1921-1929	DJIA 1949 - 1966	DJIA 1994 - March, 2000
Total Gain	+ 280.6%	+ 496.5%	+ 518.9%	+ 205.2%
Total # of Years	14 1/2 Years	8 Years, 1 Month	17 Years	5 1/2 Years
Up Years	10 Years	6 Years	13 Years	5 Years
Average Gain	+ 16.5%	+ 27.9%	+ 17.8%	+ 24.7%
Down Years	5 Years	2 Years	4 Years	0 Years
Average Loss	- 6.7%	- 1.8%	- 9.2%	N/A
Best Calendar Years	1879, + 50.2%	1928, + 48.2%	1954, + 44%	1995, + 33.4%
Worst Calendar Years	1884, - 13.5%	1923, - 3.2%	1957, - 13%	1998, + 16.1%
Rallies	7 Rallies	25 Rallies	14 Rallies	10 Rallies
Average Gain	+ 40.2%	+ 18.3%	+ 38.6%	+ 24.5%
Average Duration	16 Months	3 1/2 Months	16 Months	4 1/2 Months
Strongest Rally	+ 121.2%	+ 83.4%	+ 89%	+ 34.7%
Declines	6 Declines	25 Declines	13 Declines	10 Declines
Average Loss	- 12.7%	- 8.9%	- 17.3%	- 10.8%
Average Duration	10 Months	1 Month	6 Months	1 1/2 Months
Worst Decline	- 22.3%	- 18.7%	- 35.9%	- 20.8%
Best Group	Railroad Equip. + 880%	Automobiles, + 1076.5%	Computer Hardware, +3321%	Electronic - Instrumentation, + 1803.7%
Worst Group	Metals & Smelting - 57%	Oil Composite, + 153.0%	Bev-Alcoholic + 89.6%	Iron & Steel, - 22.1%
Average Group	+ 310%	+483.4%	+ 685.8%	+ 320.3%

INDEX